WESTERN LITERATURE
TO DANTE:
A PARENTS' GUIDE

WESTERN LITERATURE TO DANTE: A PARENTS' GUIDE

THIRD EDITION

BRUCE A. MCMENOMY, PH.D.
SCHOLARS ONLINE • 2009

PREFACE

Having designed Western Literature to Dante about a decade and a half ago, and having taught it continually since, I have been by turns charmed, excited, and puzzled to see how our students and their parents have received it.

By now, nearly three hundred have taken the course. Of those, many have told me, after four years of English study, that it was their favorite class of the sequence. The material is diverse and demanding, but it opens up many new perspectives, and it helps build a deep foundation for the later products of Western culture down to the twenty-first century. For those who choose to study Latin or Greek (or both), it provides a road-map to the authors they're reading. A number of these students have gone on to study classics or mediaeval literature in college, and they have told me that this course in particular has stood them in good stead. When I talked with a number of veterans of the course recently, and told them that I was re-thinking its composition, all of them enjoined me not to remove anything from the current reading-list. They were quite emphatic.

Others, however, have been lost from the start. I have tried to bring them along, of course, but it hasn't always been successful. For some, the whole process has clearly been disorienting and discouraging. Their parents usually find it about the same. They consider the work-load incomprehensibly large, the readings alien, and the methods obscure. Often a few months after a difficult start, they drop the course, sometimes quietly slipping away, and sometimes loudly denouncing my own faulty approach and methods.

Though of course as a teacher one likes to hear the former kind of thing more than the latter, both of these groups deserve to be heard, and I have tried to listen to them. In the process I have reached a few conclusions.

First and foremost — as so often — one size does not fit all. This is not a course for everyone. It's not so much an issue of how good a student is in some abstract sense (a reductive assessment, no matter how one approaches it), as of how a student thinks about his or her experience, and how he or she learns. By the nature of the material and the nature of the online medium, it is intensely and almost exclusively verbal, even if it is not oral. Kinesthetic learners are probably not going to do well with it. It's not that kinesthetic learners are bad — it's that they should probably look elsewhere for a curriculum that better suits their learning style.

Second is the fact that in any context, expectations — in all directions — have a great deal to do with what kind of experience one will have. If I go to see a movie but am instead treated to a live concert, I'm likely (reasonably) to feel cheated. This doesn't mean that I don't appreciate concerts — it just means that the concert isn't what I was paying for at the outset. By the same token, I'd be more than disgruntled to go to a concert and be shown a movie in its place. Expectations are fundamental. We need to be sure we are all clear about the student's expectations, the parents' expectations, and mine. Those expectations dictate certain rôles for all of us, and if we're clear on those, we'll all be happier. Yet clarifying those expectations is not always as easy as one might hope. Education — even when one is apparently able to buy it by the course — is not a mere market transaction, for at least three reasons:

First of all, it will always deal in intangibles. Despite the College Board and other well-intentioned quantifiers, nobody has ever come up with a satisfactory way of *measuring* education. It's not certain that measuring it is really possible. Nor am I persuaded that we should want to do so if it were.

Second, not everyone agrees on what success in education looks like. I have had parents complain to me that their children are struggling in the course, as if that were *ipso facto* evidence of a flaw: but while my goal is certainly not unrelieved torment, I do believe that struggle, and the ability and willingness to throw oneself into struggle without any guarantee of victory, is an important part of both intellectual and moral education.

Finally, teaching itself is not, I believe, so much a matter of the conveyance of material as it is the formation of a dynamic personal relationship, of which learning is almost a by-product. If I buy a gallon of milk and five tomatoes at the local grocery store, I hand the clerk my money and walk away with exactly what I determined to buy. The job is done. Assuming the milk is not sour and the tomatoes are not wormy, I'm satisfied; if there are defects, they are objectively verifiable and we can reach an accommodation. Learning, however, is not so closed a transaction. As a teacher, I cannot unilaterally bring it about. I can help parents and students create a context in which the right materials are at hand; I can ask leading questions; I can suggest answers to those questions. But the student must bring about his or her own learning. Education is something one must do for oneself, like eating or sleeping. It's part and parcel of the inward formation of the person, and it cannot be bestowed upon a passive recipient, willy-nilly. It may be tended by as many gardeners as you like, but ultimately it has to grow in the native soil of the student's mind and soul. Though the materials we work with are the common heritage of Western culture and of the world, each of us can tackle them only by making them uniquely our own. One can admire that fact or one can deplore it (I've had parents do both), but one cannot avoid it. Anyone claiming otherwise is selling snake oil.

Accordingly, I have prepared this book in order to ease parents' initial process of discernment ("Is this the right course for us?"), and to enable better follow-through once they've made that decision ("How can we make this work?"). I can say that if you agree to its terms from the start, and are willing to make a commitment to the rôles here outlined, you will go into the process with your eyes open, and you will not be taken by surprise. I can further say that if you follow through with the suggested materials, and assess your student's progress at home in a timely way, we'll all be a lot happier with what results. If you're not willing or able to agree to those terms, we're probably better off not getting into this in the first place. Of course I hope you will agree, and will find the course challenging and interesting, and that your children will find it as intriguing as many of their predecessors have.

CONTENTS

INTRODUCTION

This course is aptly but optimistically named "Western Literature to Dante". It attempts to cover in the space of thirty-five weeks of online chat the chief creative endeavors of about 2500 years. It cannot pretend to be more than the sketchiest survey.

I am nonetheless convinced that such a survey is valuable. It provides a number of reference-points, and introduces literary landmarks that are both valuable in their own right, and gauges by which to measure others. From here, a student can go back over and across the field with increasing freedom, and will find (I hope) that the lay of the land is ever more familiar.

A student who has completed this course will have read more literature of the pre-modern world than all but a tiny handful of American high school students, and will also have acquired a small but sturdy analytical vocabulary that can be applied to other works, both ancient and modern.

It is beyond the scope of this book to mount a defense of the reading of classical and mediaeval literature: if you have it in your hands, you are probably already persuaded of its value in any case. What I can add to that reflection here is the suggestion that anything that's of real value is probably going to require some real effort to acquire. Learning this material — especially encountering it for the first time — is difficult. It has proven tough for some of the best students I've ever taught (interestingly, often tougher for them than for weaker students). But as I mentioned elsewhere, many of them said afterward that it was their favorite course out of four years of literary study. A number of them have gone on to major in classical or mediaeval studies in college.

It is tough. I'm not trying to hide that. It's not a terribly hard course to pass, if a student will do the reading and apply sufficient effort to the matter at hand. It doesn't require enormous brilliance as such. But to get its full benefit, one must put in some sustained work and some real thought — not just to pass exams, (which are fairly easy, in fact) but to encompass and engage the literature — to make it one's own. What one can get here, I believe, is not merely a list of facts about classical and mediaeval literature (which could be picked up in a variety of contexts), but the beginning of a view from inside it — a glimpse through eyes other than our own, from a far corner of what is nevertheless in many ways our own culture. Those eyes sometimes see more clearly than do those of our contemporaries, and sometimes they don't. But if we take the view advisedly, we are not ourselves restricted by its limitations, and we may well be enlarged and enhanced by its broadened perspectives.

Before You Start:
Skills and Other Preparation

Any course begins with certain expectations, and all but the most elementary courses presume some kind of previous learning on the part of the student. This is not in all respects an elementary course. The students who come to us are of wildly divergent backgrounds, and I've discovered that it's not safe to assume that anyone has encountered anything in particular. So here is an outline of the kind of preparation that will help a student do well in this course. It's a guideline. Probably nobody comes to us with all these tools in place, and that's understandable: after all, part of the purpose of the educational process is to sharpen such skills as you go. At the same time, if *all* of it looks like strange territory, perhaps it would be wiser to take another year to prepare.

The Ability to Read Well and Extensively

The first and perhaps most obvious requirement is that the student be able to read well. This is as much a matter of stamina as of technical virtuosity. There is simply too much reading for a student who cannot continuously read for more than ten minutes at a time — whether that's because he finds the process exhausting or because he finds that he just can't sit still any longer than that.

In practical terms, there's also a balance between the precision required of a careful reader and an overly fastidious approach that will cause the whole process to crumble under its own weight. A student should be able to recognize when he is understanding what's going on.

Being unclear on a word here or there is normal, especially when reading literature written two thousand years ago and half a world away.
Learning any language involves developing the ability to go on in
some confidence despite the occasional uncertainty. At the same time,
an alarm bell should go off when the words are just floating by and
nothing seems to be making sense any more. At that point, one needs
to apply the brakes and take stock. Often, just looking a few key terms
up will break up the log-jam — assuming the student can identify
which terms to look up. This is something with which parents can
help, though I am certainly willing to field questions that go beyond
the obvious.

The reading-load for Western Literature to Dante varies considerably over the course of the year — being at its maximum for the three
anchoring authors, Homer, Vergil, and Dante — and there are a few
weeks that will require about two hundred pages of reading (narrative
text with a story). If that's clearly impossible, consider carefully
whether this is what you want to do. If it's just likely to be a bit of a
stretch, it may be a stretch worth trying. Nobody grows without a challenge.

A BASIC HISTORICAL OUTLINE

This is not a history course, but it's taught on relentlessly historical
principles. As noted already, its material covers a stretch of well over
two thousand years, and a good deal of the point of the course is ena-
bling the student to put these pieces into relationship with each other,
and to understand their connections.

For that reason, it's necessary for a student to have some sense of
what happened in world history, and to be able to handle chronology

in its broadest terms. I'm not looking for deep and analytical under-standing — that typically comes at a later stage. But I am looking for an acquaintance with the basic outlines of historical events so that I'm not always having to clarify what is meant by archaic Greece or Impe-rial Rome. There have been students who have told me on exams that the Roman poet Horace was a contemporary of Augustus, and there-fore lived around A.D. 800, or that Augustine (a Christian saint) lived in the fifth century B.C. This is disturbing for several reasons. First of all, it makes me doubt that any of the rest of the material has made any better sense; second, it suggests that the student has not bothered to draw any inferences: if Jesus was born in the reign of Augustus, as Luke tells us, his contemporaries are unlikely to be alive eight hundred years later. Nor could those who followed him in the Christian faith have preceded him by half a millennium.

Gaining control here is mostly a matter of establishing enough points of reference that one knows where one is from moment to mo-ment — and those can be acquired during the course if need be. But if the student doesn't have at least a few historical anchors, this requires immediate remedial attention: work with your student on this from day one until it's under control. There's an appendix containing a time-line of the major events of this course — literary events and major world-historical signposts. Mastering even these few will help a lot.

SOME INTRODUCTORY MYTHOLOGY

I have for years recommended that students read Edith Hamilton's *Mythology* or Bulfinch's *Mythology* over the summer before they begin this course, and that they read some abbreviated introduction to the

Arthurian mythos over the Christmas break (I particularly mentioned Sidney Lanier's somewhat dated *The Boy's King Arthur*, but there are several others that work as well). Neither of these is required: the way enrollment goes, it's virtually impossible to insist on it. But just as knowing your way around the historical landscape and the chronological material is essential, so also having some concept of the basic stories and cast of characters is very beneficial. Once the course is underway, it's probably too late for remediation on this score — the student is already in the midst of wrestling with so many stories that throwing another narrative into the mix is unlikely to add clarity. But I have found that those for whom all the names are not strange are the ones who grasp the stories most quickly and effectively. This is probably too obvious to require discussion, but I do definitely encourage students to do something about it when the time is right.

THE ABILITY TO WRITE CLEARLY AND EFFICIENTLY

This question is something of a bottomless pit. Nobody writes well enough, ever. Everyone would like to improve. I know I would. But this course definitely requires the ability to produce rational continuous prose under pressure. It's not itself a writing course; we have a separate writing program that can help develop these skills while the course is underway. I can help a little in comments on exams, but often that proves too little, too late. At a minimum a student should come to the course ready and able to *explain* something clearly in writing. I'm not looking for Pulitzer Prize writing and I don't score exams primarily on the quality of the prose. At the same time, though, I can't give points to answers I can't understand, or arguments that don't argue, or essays that just end abruptly before they have really said anything.

This is probably the skill that most varies at this age. Some students in the fourth or fifth grade can produce remarkably lucid prose; others cannot do so by the eighth grade. Assess this carefully; if necessary, consult me on the matter. It will make a difference in your student's appreciation of the course.

STEPPING BACK TO LOOK AT SOMETHING OBJECTIVELY

This is desirable, but, like the previous item, something of a receding goal. Objective, clear analysis is a hard-won commodity, and I certainly do not expect a student to come into the course with it all in place. Still, a student who is unwilling to treat certain things objectively will probably find a number of things in the course that will upset him or her. Scholars Online is a Christian organization by design and in fact — but not everything we read in this course is Christian material. (This should surprise no one, especially when we're dealing with material written before Christ, but I have encountered students and parents who were apparently shocked and offended by the fact.) The ability to sift such writings for what they contain of worth, and to understand and imaginatively and provisionally to enter into alternate world-views, is organic to the functioning of the course.

THE ABILITY TO ENGAGE WITH THE MATERIAL

This is almost the antithesis of the foregoing: whereas it's necessary to step *back* and exercise objectivity, it's also necessary to step *forward* into the work somewhat, to engage with it, strive with it, and try to understand it as honestly and clearly as possible on its own terms. For some students this comes naturally; for others, it requires a real exercise of faith, and it can be a frightening prospect. The end result, we hope, will be the ability to see and think clearly while at the same time entering into the matter sympathetically.

PEDAGOGICAL GOALS

DIGGING OUT THE AUTHOR'S MEANING

Most of the reading we have to do in life, in any context, demands that we get through a lot of material in a little time, with substantial, even if imperfect, understanding. Whether we're dealing with a literary product or an interoffice memo, though, we have to read efficiently and discern accurately what the author is driving at. That may seem obvious, but I still encounter many students for whom this is the primary challenge. So it has always been and remains one of the primary goals of the course.

In other words, we're not looking for extreme subtleties and we're not looking for trick wordings. We're not trying to do anything very high-brow or in a lot of ways what people sometimes think of as "literary". Close reading — taking the phrases apart and looking minutely at the meanings and inter-related parts with a microscope — is an important technique, and I certainly don't mean to slight it. In fact, that's one of the main pedagogical goals behind the English Literature course (which normally follows this one). But it's not my goal here. For *this* course my main hope is that the student will be able to read large works and understand basically what they're about. Specific and more particular literary themes — there are a few we cover — are mostly identified in class discussions.

There are a few reasons for this — some of them having to do with the way we approach the process, and some of them to do with the nature of the material itself. First, it certainly seems more fundamentally *important* to be able to grasp the central idea than to fish for the abstruse details at the margins, and so it makes more sense to start by mastering that skill. Though most of our students have been reading for some years by the time they get to us, few of them have ever been forced to plow through quite so much material in such a way, and to extract from it the central kernel of idea.

Moreover, any energy expended on close reading of translated texts is largely wasted. I will happily go through these works with students when they're able to tackle them — Plato in Greek III, Homer in Greek IV, and Euripides in Greek V; Vergil in Latin IV, and Catullus and Horace in Latin V, and others as occasion arises. But to attempt to draw any very sophisticated conclusions about the verbal artistry of the author, when one cannot see the author's words, is an exercise in self-deception. That's another reason we defer close reading for English Literature — there we're confronting the texts in their language and in our own.

The ability to read efficiently, with an eye always to the main matter, is the most important skill a student can carry away from this course. This is why I have always adamantly refused to produce a study guide for the course (this manual for parents coming as close as anything I've done to date). It's not that I don't want to do the work to prepare a list of terms and concepts to be mastered. I could certainly do that — with less trouble than it has taken to write this handbook, to be sure. It might improve measurable student performance, and it would surely make some people feel a lot more secure about the course. But in so doing, I would also be short-circuiting this most important of the course's pedagogical goals — helping the student to learn how to manage this distillation for himself. If a student learns how to do this, he's acquired something extremely valuable that will not be dislodged easily by this or any subsequent kind of study. Failing this, on the other hand, mere mastery of a list of names and dates is of very limited value. The important thing is for the student to do his or her own reading, and to draw his or her *own* conclusions about what is important. Not all of those conclusions will be correct, and not all will agree with mine. But learning *how* to draw them is a fundamentally different process from merely mastering someone else's list of conclusions, just as knowing how to cook is different from knowing how to eat. Learning to cook is hard, and leads one out of insecurity through a process of iterative refinement and improvement. It's seldom as satisfying from moment to moment as merely eating, and at times it's downright frustrating. But it's worthwhile — because if you can cook, eventually you get to where you can eat without having someone else feed you. If you're good at it, you can routinely make things that you actually *want* to eat.

THE BIG QUESTIONS RAISED BY THIS LITERATURE

These works of literature are considered enduring classics of the world for one main reason: they raise questions and speak to people about those questions through every generation. They are bigger, in a sense, than the local situation and culture that begot them. Anyone who has any claim to the rudiments of education should ultimately have wrestled with these ideas and issues. The author of Genesis and Exodus confronts us with the question, "What is our obligation to our God, and how do we have a relationship with Him?" Homer asks us, "What does it mean to be human?" Aeschylus asks whether there is any end to be found to a cycle of violence and revenge, and whether civil due process can help us set aside ancient blood-feuds. Sophocles asks us how we can reasonably balance the demands of the state and the demands of our faith and conscience. Euripides questions whether the solution Aeschylus offers is really strong enough to endure against ancient hatreds and the apparent indifference or even pettiness of the gods. Plato asks where our consciousness comes from, and suggests a model of moral behavior that continues to challenge us. Lucretius offers a purely materialistic model of the universe, suggesting that religion is a ruse and a delusion. Caesar seems to legitimize the will to power of the "great man"; Vergil writes a sort of epic at the end of a period of civil war, and, using the vocabulary of Homer, stands the Caesarian model on its head, asking whether any society can endure on those terms — effectively raising once again (and not for the last time) the questions of Homer and Aeschylus before him: Can we be human? Can we overcome the baser promptings of our nature? The writers of the Gospel come onto the scene and give a split answer to Vergil's question: our nature is as flawed and fallen as he had feared (probably worse) but there is a path of redemption.

One could go on — but you can look into these things more closely in the week-by-week account of the class material below. My point here, however, is that these are questions that won't go away. They are the questions you will find in any given issue of a world newspaper, every day. The Zionist and the Islamic fundamentalist and the committed Christian are all wrestling with the questions of how to enter and maintain a relationship with God. Every day our courts try to find a pragmatic way to resolve conflict. People who argue for or against putting the Ten Commandments on the walls of schoolroom or the words "under God" into the Pledge of Allegiance are asking a close cousin of the question that troubled Antigone in Sophocles' play. Marxism and other materialist philosophies have assailed us repeatedly throughout the last century, and have at times seemed close to claiming a practical victory. But these things are nothing new. The era of the great dictators and the Nietzchean will to power — the ability to exercise the power of the will and destroy their opposition — neither began with Nietzsche nor ended with Hitler. The nineteenth century saw Napoleon, and the late twentieth saw Pol Pat, Idi Amin, and Saddam Hussein — all of them cut roughly from the same cloth. The breed seems to show no sign of imminent extinction. The ancient Greeks and Romans knew them as well as we do, and Plato discussed them as lucidly as anyone has since. These ancient authors came up with some ideas and conclusions that we may agree with or not: we'd be mindless drones to agree with them all, but we'd be blockheads to ignore them altogether, too. If someone has managed to ask so many of the right questions, it's likely he will at least occasionally have stumbled across some of the right answers.

BUILDING THE HISTORICAL FRAMEWORK

Part of the point of this course — it is, after all, a kind of survey — is to provide a sense of the "lay of the land". What does it look like? Who was doing what, when, and why? These are issues of both space and time. It very much helps for the student to have an atlas or at least a convenient set of basic maps of Europe and the Mediterranean available. Where is Athens? Where was Troy? Where is Rome? What is the difference in their situation? When did they exercise power? What happens to culture in the Middle Ages? Where does the center of cultural gravity move? Why?

The other thing that needs to be appreciated about the scope of this course is the sheer vastness of the time it takes in. It stretches, as we have pointed out, over a period of about two and a half millennia: one may sweepingly dismiss it all as "antique" — but let's be clear about what it is. Look at the time-line at the end of this book. The earliest works we study (the Old Testament and Homer) are about three times as far removed in time from the latest (Dante's *Divine Comedy*) as the last is removed from us. The stretches of time involved here are enormous. They dwarf, in simple duration, everything that has happened since — the material we are inclined to think of as making up the bulk of history.

Accordingly, some of the benefit of this course, it is hoped, is just the building of a framework and a sense of perspective, in time and space, in which these things can be appreciated.

PICKING UP THE NARRATIVE OUTLINE

Some of the point of this course (and this is arguably an outgrowth of the first goal — just getting the author's point) has to do with discerning the narrative outline — not just getting the main propositional points that the author might want to make, but also discerning how a story is shaped, and how it accomplishes what it does. What *is* story, and why do we respond to it? Is it important? Does it serve as anything more than a medium for philosophical, social, or political ideas? Is it mere entertainment? I shall perhaps tip my hand a bit here by saying that I believe story is a critical part of who and what we are: I don't think that people can understand themselves individually or collectively without having a firm grasp on what their story is, and it's worth reflecting on how that works. I think that as a culture we dismiss story to our intellectual and spiritual peril, and if we determine that high literature is entirely about the transmission of abstract ideas, we banish story to the realm of the television drama — but it will win in the long run.

PICKING UP THEMES BEYOND THE NARRATIVE OUTLINE

At the same time, we *can* also look for the themes that stand behind and inform the narrative — not because they are necessarily the *purpose* of the narrative, but because they are the common currency of the author's thought. They are the questions the author is asking about, and the terms in which he both frames the questions and expects to see them answered. If we read Homer armed exclusively with a twentieth-century thematic sense, and fail to figure out his vocabulary and what's important to him, then we are probably going to miss much of what he's saying. To see Achilles as a type of the modern soldier fighting for a nation-state is to scramble the picture completely. It's similarly misleading to read Vergil without discerning how he both picks up Homer's themes and how he seems to be rejecting Homer's answers, at least for his own day and age. To read Dante at face value, or without knowing some of the questions Vergil raises, is going to be a source of confusion too.

CULTIVATION OF A CRITICAL QUESTIONING ATTITUDE

Finally, I would hope that any student would acquire a questioning, discriminating attitude. I don't insist that any student *like* anything we read here. I suspect almost every student will find at least something to like, and that almost every student will probably find something to dislike as well. That's okay. I merely ask that they read, learn, and reflect, and that they not be too dismissive of anything. These questions that are raised here are without doubt going to be with us for a good long time yet, and they deserve recognition and recollection.

THEMES AND TOPICS

THE HERO

One narrative topic that runs through nearly the whole length of the material we read is the concept of the hero. By that I don't merely mean a protagonist, but someone who struggles (frequently at the ultimate cost of his life) for something he believes in. I have made this a central thematic element in the course for a few reasons. First of all, it's useful to look at it precisely because it's a very broad theme. Almost every culture that has made an enduring mark on the world has had a notion of heroism, so it supplies a useful point of comparison for us. We can characterize the literature at least in part by how it treats the hero.

In a larger and more nebulous — but no less important — sense, I think heroism is worth examining on its own terms for what it is, and as a model for our own behavior. We live in a culture that has largely been drained of any notion of heroism; irony and skepticism have conspired, in a sense, to erode the modern world's view of the hero, especially when times are reasonably good and the worst things to happen to us are scandals and instances of hypocrisy. The figure of the hero does, however, re-emerge in darker times of stress — war, catastrophe, or the like. The rhetoric following the events of Sept. 11, 2001 brought the word to the surface in a hurry, and we heard it more in public discourse than we had for the previous decade. Much of that talk was glib and politically opportunistic, but there was more than a little truth to it as well. I believe that the concept of heroism deserves re-examination and rehabilitation in several ways.

In looking at the hero from the Old Testament through mediaeval romance, I have largely focused on the question, "What motivates these people? What are they doing, and why? For what are they willing to make sacrifices?" The results are, I think, illuminating in both their variety and their consistency. The driving force behind the Homeric hero is vastly different from that motivating the Patriarch of the Old Testament or the Roman hero. We attempt loosely to catalogue those distinctions. At the same time, in almost every case the hero is someone who *does* risk himself — his life, and perhaps his very identity — for something he sees as being of transcendent value. Sometimes it is only the immortality of his own personal fame (*e.g.* the Homeric *kleos*: see glossary); sometimes it is the good of the community or state (e.g. the hero of Livy's *Ab urbe condita*); sometimes it is obedience to a moral imperative (*e.g.*, Antigone); sometimes it's the personal commitment a personal God (*e.g.*, Abraham, Paul, Augustine). But it's a value for which the hero is willing to risk everything he has and is.

In an age that questions any kind of higher purpose, and commends material gratification to us at every turn, the heroes of the past — pagan and Christian, real or fictional (some of each represented here) — all stand as witnesses to *their* cultures' aspirations to something higher, and a reminder that we can do better too.

Forms of Presentation

One concept that some students acquire only with difficulty is that literature is not *one* thing but many — it comes in a variety of shapes and sizes and forms on the one hand, and with a remarkable variety of content on the other. For some, we have to begin with the notion that "poetry" and "rhyme" are not identical categories: in fact, before modern times, rhyme was at most an infrequent feature of poetry, and anything like regular end-rhyme was considered a defect in classical Greek and Latin.

The problem doesn't get any simpler after we've solved that, though. In ancient and mediaeval literature, in particular, there is often an implicit link between literary form and content — but the connection is neither absolute, nor is it often preserved in translation. Greek and Roman epic, for example, was without exception written in dactylic hexameter (six feet of the general pattern long-short-short). This rule was sufficiently iron-clad that something written in a different form would have been considered to be non-epic by definition — it would *have* to be something else. On the other hand, not all hexametric poetry was epic: the form was also used for didactic poetry — discussions of such things as when to plant (Hesiod's *Works and Days*) and the nature of the physical universe (Lucretius' *De rerum natura*). And yet later works that are commonly classified as epics (*The Song of Roland, The Nibelungenlied, Beowulf*, etc.) are in fact in a variety of different forms, none of them hexametric. They are, however, always poetry of *some* sort. An epic in prose is not an epic. It might veer toward being a saga, though that (prose) form has its own peculiar features and restrictions. Of course in Hollywood advertising, the word "epic" has been diluted into a synonym for "big", and can then be freely applied to film. Language is a slippery thing.

To complicate the problem further, virtually no *translation* of even Greek and Roman epic retains its original form: some are in poetry and some are in prose, but very few (*e.g.*, Lattimore's Homer) are really in the original metric structure. (Longfellow tried quantitative hexameter in *Evangeline*, but it has not been considered an unmixed success.) Some (*e.g.*, Pope's *Iliad* or Dryden's *Aeneid*) rhyme with a jingle that would have alarmed Homer or Vergil.

What are we to make of all this? The ancient world assumed that there was some kind of rational connection between form and content. If you wanted to write about wars and mighty deeds, you'd use the hexameter; if you wanted to complain about your best friend's death or about how your girlfriend had abandoned you, you'd use elegiac couplets. Later writers have often deliberately flouted such conventions in the sake of interest and style, but still — whether one believes that there is or ought to be such an intimate connection between form and content — the question deserves to be explored, and the student needs to learn to recognize the various forms and the content-types that correspond with them. Accordingly we spend a certain amount of time discussing how various ancient and mediaeval forms of literature arose, and also how those forms can accommodate themselves to the substance they have to deliver. While one *can* write a play in limericks, in other words, the medium is almost certainly going to restrict the playwright's options a good deal, and his chances of writing a convincing tragedy in such a form will be virtually nil.

Narrative Techniques and Analytical Categories

The number of ways in which an author can arrange his material is virtually limitless. But certain patterns emerge, and learning to recognize them is likely to enhance our appreciation of what the author is doing and why; it also affords further opportunities for us to compare the works of different authors.

I have made no systematic attempt to be exhaustive in this department, but I have tried to show students how to recognize a handful of what seem to me to be the most important narrative constructions. Where they occur, I have tried to point out such things as the *aristeia* in Homeric poetry (see glossary).

In particular I have tried to explore the various methods authors have developed of enclosing or encapsulating one story within another. In this latter class, I would include such things as the narrated story within a story (for example, the poet reciting tales in the *Odyssey*, or Odysseus telling his own story), and in particular the *ecphrasis* (or *ekphrasis*), a peculiar ancient technique (but still being used in contemporary modern fiction) of expressing or referring to another story by an extended description of a physical object (usually a pictorial artifact) that contains the elements of that story. By seeing how a range of authors do this, one can appreciate the subtlety of the tool for what it is — and when it arises in a modern work like Melville's *Moby-Dick* or Eco's *The Name of the Rose*, we are better prepared to see how it works.

STRUCTURES OF THOUGHT AND WORLD-VIEW

Any literary or artistic product will inevitably say a good deal about how the author and his culture thought and viewed the world. These issues are often reduced to trivialities by people with an axe to grind, but they are complex questions that deserve respectful handling. An unbiased comparison of a variety of literary products can tell us a good deal about such things. When the *Iliad* contrasts the fate of a man's soul with the fate of the man himself, we don't have to probe too deeply to realize that the two were seen as basically distinct. When Aeschylus

gives us his dark choruses, detailing the bloody deaths of small animals, but apparently also referring to the human situation in his play, it
tells us something about how he saw the coherence of reality between
humanity and nature, of such things as blood-sacrifice and blood-guilt,
and the inter-relationship of nature, the gods, and mankind.

By the same token, when Plato's Socrates relentlessly asks questions
about abstract concepts, he is expressing both an abiding belief in the
enduring *reality* of those abstractions, and also an unshakeable faith
that objective truth really is out there to be known. He is telling us,
moreover, that dialectical inquiry is the right way of tracking it down.
A Christian writer whose faith is rooted in a firm belief in the Resurrection will view every other aspect of life, from moral categories to inci-
dental matters, differently. The cases multiply: just by observing how
an argument or story is set out, and what kinds of things are taken for
granted, one can learn a remarkable number of things about almost
any author. As one goes on to compare these from one writer to another, a subtle contour emerges — a contour that defines the interior
history of our culture and civilization.

How Language Shapes
and is Shaped by Thought

We all realize that language — almost any use of language, other
than the purely musical — expresses some kind of thought. It does not
follow, of course, that all such thought is intrinsically profound, or
even that it is valid or rational (indeed, it hardly could be, as long as
people can state contradictory propositions in language); but it is an
expression of thought nonetheless.

What is not as well appreciated is the fact that language in turn shapes the thoughts expressed in that language. Neither exercises absolute primacy; our minds apparently work at or beyond the limits of language at least part of the time, but they also drift along pre-established patterns of words and phrases we've already heard and used. The result is a reciprocal dynamic of thought and expression that defies easy analysis, but deserves consideration.

The echoing structures of the Hebrew Psalms, for example, bespeak but also probably helped create and reinforce a mental pattern of binary analysis of reality in the Israel of 1000 B.C. — but they also help shape a similar rhetoric of binary opposition among the mediaeval monastics who recited those Psalms every day, in a different language, two millennia later. The formulae of Homeric composition suggest a kind of modular approach to the raw ingredients of experience, in which pieces larger than individual words are interchangeable.

It is in acknowledgment of this complexity that I have included in the curriculum Erich Auerbach's *Mimesis: The Representation of Reality in Western Literature*. The work is, I freely admit, far beyond the ability of the average high school student to master thoroughly. For that reason, while I use it as the basis for class discussion or as an ingredient in optional questions on exams, I seldom examine students on it very thoroughly. I continue to use it, though, because a surprising number of students through the years have shown that they are able to grasp what Auerbach is talking about, and the results are astounding. For further elaboration of this, I can do no better than to refer the reader to the book itself; no attempt to paraphrase its content here would be worth our time or trouble. I consider it one of the greatest works of literary scholarship of the twentieth century.

It should be said, however (especially in view of the fact that Scholars Online's program is explicitly Christian) that Auerbach was not himself Christian; he was a German Jew who had the perspicacity to flee Germany in the late 1930s. After spending the bulk of World War II in Istanbul, he came to the United States, where he continued to work at the Princeton Institute for Advanced Studies until his death. I have had some parents and some students object to some of Auerbach's comments and some of his assumptions: please understand that I give this book to this class not because I endorse everything Auerbach has to say (I don't) but because his work models a certain kind of literary thinking that is growing rarer every day: it is faithful to the text, and it asks probing questions that have real and legitimate bearing on the way literature works and how it says anything to us. Like everything else in this course, it needs to be weighed with a certain amount of discretion. Parental guidance is likely to be particularly useful in dealing with difficulties here.

HOW TEXTS MEAN WHAT THEY MEAN

Toward the end of the course, as we are preparing to tackle Dante's *Divine Comedy*, we consider some particularly tricky ideas about *how* texts, literary or otherwise, are able to convey meaning, and how they can express ideas on literal and symbolic levels. Our analysis is largely an outgrowth of ideas expressed by Thomas Aquinas, but in turn rooted in some much older discussions between Antiochene and Alexandrian Christians about the nature of Biblical exegesis. This is one of the fundamental questions of scriptural analysis, and insofar as students are able to grasp the subtlety involved, I think it's a very useful question to consider. Once again, I don't, certainly, prescribe one approach over another: how one tackles the question will inevitably vary in accord with the way the student views scripture. But the question is nevertheless of enormous importance to any thinking Christian.

Practical Methods and Techniques

On more than one occasion I have been asked by students various versions of the question, "How do I study all this?" For a few, I think, the question is rhetorical; it is meant to indicate that the whole thing is just an amorphous mass, impossible to learn, and by asking the question they absolve themselves of the obligation to try. Here I'm addressing the other, larger, class of students — those who really want to know the answer. There *are* things that can be done to make this course more efficient — and in fact, some of them will make the process of studying *anything* more efficient.

Study in General

Study requires faith, courage, and stamina.

It requires faith because one does not always perceive the benefit of all this hard work right away. The view from the trenches is limited, and generally devoid of strategic perspective. One labors on in the hope and faith that the promised reward is worth the effort. I'd like to be able to say that everyone who has emerged on the other side of the process agrees that it *has* been worthwhile. Alas, I cannot. I think that it is, and so do most who have completed it — but not everyone has or will.

It requires courage because in almost no other human enterprise is one so constantly stepping out from the known into the unknown. That's what learning is about, of course — but it entails certain personal and emotional risks, and it's only right to tip the hat to those who have the gumption to do it.

And it requires raw stamina, because it is usually just plain old hard work. For a very few it proves easy, but eventually even they reach a point where it is not. It's at this boundary of the understanding that most of the real learning takes place, though — so this is not the point at which to bail out. It's here, too, that the character of the student is tested and refined.

There are rewards. Nobody who has never struggled with something can know the triumph of overcoming an obstacle. There's a deep satisfaction that comes with that. And there's a simple gratification that comes from knowing and understanding how certain things fit together. Learning can be fun.

At the same time, however, it's not *guaranteed* to be fun. For most, it's hard but fun. For some it's both difficult and unpleasant. I'm not sure I can do anything about the unpleasantness — that's largely a function of the attitude the student brings along with him to the enterprise — but I think I can provide some guidelines.

As so often, expectations are a key issue here. Be realistic about what this is going to require. I have received panicky letters from parents, saying things like, "My child is spending over half an hour a day on this material, and still isn't getting 100%!" I can only answer that yes, that's very likely true. The course is *intended* to take more than half an hour a day. For most students, it's going to take somewhere between an hour and a half and two hours a day. This is not a miscalculation on my part, nor is it, I think, an urealistic expectation. If one were attending a conventional school, one would have an hour a day in class, followed up with half an hour to an hour of homework. This is a tough college-prep course, and it lays the groundwork for the rest of the English sequence. It's going to take time. If you disagree with that approach, though, you are probably looking at the wrong course. It's better that we resolve that now.

The other thing that needs to be addressed early is the significance of scores or grades. I score these exams on my own scale, not on a curve. This is not a trivial beginning course where one can easily quantify the percentage of material a student has learned (as one could, for example, if the subject were the multiplication table). In a course at this level, any teacher could probably write an exam that nobody would pass, or an exam that everyone could pass. From *my* point of view, if a student gets an average of 50% on my exams, he's passing. This is not because I'm dumbing anything down: it's because that's the way I've written the exams. Accordingly, parents who are indignant because their kids are not getting scores in the nineties, when they got scores in the nineties somewhere else, are just missing the point.

The other fact here, however, is that, while I'm eager to see every student succeed, and would be thrilled to have a class full of scores ranging from 98 to 100, I truly believe that the value of the course is not in the scores, but in the *substance* of the course. On that measure, therefore, if you believe that your son or daughter is getting something worthwhile from the course, while pulling down an average of 30%, *that's fine with me*. In the last analysis, you are the teacher of record: I am not. You can assign to that 30% any value you like. I don't think less of you or of him or her for that. We get kids with very different preparation, and the playing field is never level. But I've admitted students who've failed one year into the next year's course. Sometimes they struggle along and barely pass there, too — and then sometimes in the third year, they come alive, as if a light has gone on. Has the intervening time been well spent? Some of them seemed to think so.

How does one account for this? I don't know. Certainly not by a cascade of mere numbers or letters on a transcript. Perhaps some critical piece of understanding just clicked into place. Perhaps it was divine prompting. The Lord is gracious, but so far He hasn't seen fit to give me a plan ahead of time. Doubtless He has His reasons.

All that being said, I can perhaps pare back the amount of time the course will require — certainly reduce the amount of time spent in wasted motion. When that's out of the way, there's more payoff for a given amount of study. What is required at the outset and throughout the course is some careful discernment and supervision from the parents.

TWO DIFFERENT KINDS OF STUDY

This course, like most other courses, requires two different kinds of learning and understanding. Distinguishing the two will greatly aid in the task of mastery.

In the first place, it requires the raw acquisition of factual material. Frankly, there's a fair amount of this to be learned; some of it is more historical than strictly literary. Especially a student who has not hitherto built a very reliable mental historical framework will find that this occupies a fair amount of time. This kind of mastery also requires very particular kinds of study skills — the ability to read carefully, and several kinds of drill, which will be discussed below.

The course also requires the ability to *use* what has been learned — to put the terms into context, to manipulate ideas, and to dig past the surface for the underlying themes and to explore intrinsic problems; this is a reflective, questioning process that is not easy to encapsulate, but this is what we're attempting to model and promote in class discussions. Insofar as it can be studied at all, it requires a completely different approach. Mastery here is less easily quantified and (perhaps for that reason) less easily achieved; but it absolutely depends on getting the factual materials right to start with — so we'll start there.

READING

Everything in this course begins with the written word. A regular program of orderly reading is essential. Make it a high priority to ensure at the beginning of the year that *regular time is set aside daily for reading*. This is the first and most important step you can take. You may already know that early in the day is good for this, or you may know that time after dinner works best. Whatever it is, adhere to it, and only deviate from the pattern deliberately and for good reason.

When the course begins, check up right away — from the first week on (*i.e.,* after the first class) you should be able to find out from your student how the reading is going. If there are problems here, you will be able to find out about that a lot faster than I will. I ask in class for questions, but the bewildered student is also often somewhat intimidated, despite my own best efforts to appear friendly and approachable, and is usually the last one to ask for help when he or she needs it. If there are problems in getting through the reading, *let me know immediately*. I can't alter the reading schedule at this point, since it's more or less built for the whole year, but I can perhaps offer some more specific suggestions than these for how to get through it.

The biggest problem I've run into in terms of reading has been the student who simply goes on through a piece of text, mentally (or even aurally or subvocally) hitting every word, but drifting on for pages without really knowing what in the world is going on. This is not a problem unique to slow students. Everyone who reads has probably encountered it at one time or another; I know I have. The best remedy to this is almost certainly some question and answer — ask what's going on in each part of the story. Bear in mind that *most* of what we read this year is narrative literature, and therefore *has* a story. There are some exceptions, but the big pieces of reading are narrative. The philosophical and literary-theoretical writings, or even the lyrical poetry, tend to be doled out in much smaller doses. When we are involved in a story, though, we can, for the most part, follow the thread; when we're engrossed in it, we can even usually go along at a pretty good clip. Making that connection is essential.

If your student has problems of this sort, I'd suggest a couple of possible remedies. The first is writing for himself or herself a simple summary. If something is divided into chunks, come up with a name for each chunk, and write a *precis* of each — no more than a few sentences, describing what's happening. Of course that's going to vary with the size of the chunk: if one writes a summary of each chapter of Exodus, one is going to have a much more detailed account than one will get by writing an equivalent amount about each of the eight books of Homer one has to read in a week.

If that doesn't prove practical, perhaps conversation will do the trick. Ask your student to *tell* you the story, in broadest outline terms. This provides three distinct benefits. First of all, it's a great diagnostic. You'll find out in a day or two whether the readings are clicking or not — a long time before I'll find out, after the first exam. Second, some students are able to understand it better once they have put it into their own words — this is a well-attested phenomenon in all learning. And finally, going to speech brings another sense (hearing) into play, and reinforces the sensory mechanisms that will promote retention of the material over the year that follows.

DRILL

To many students and many parents, "drill" is a dirty word. It's associated with everything that's tedious and grinding about the educational process. But it's still with us in every successful educational system, no matter how enlightened our processes become, because in fact there is no form of learning that does not require the acquisition of *some* amount of factual material, which must merely be learned in its raw condition. It's not a matter of wisdom, and it's not a matter of crushing the spirits of children: it's just the way the world works. Fact is the basic material — the stuff of our discourse. Without it, there is no articulation in what we do, and the whole mechanism becomes a foggy blur. The trick is acquiring it quickly and efficiently so that one can move on to the more interesting bits.

So what's the best way to drill? From elementary school through graduate school, I had occasion over and over again to resort to the humble flash card. I used flash cards for studying the multiplication tables in the earliest grades, and I used them later to master historical facts and to acquire foreign language vocabulary, or to train myself in the complexities of Greek and Latin lyric meters in graduate school. As students in many of my classes will attest, I still fervently recommend them as one of the best educational tools ever invented.

Flash cards are terrific in part *because* they're low-tech. You never have to boot a flash card; it never crashes. It's cheap, it doesn't need an operating system upgrade, and it gets out of the way when you're done with it. This latter point is probably the easiest to overlook, but it's central to drilling effectively on anything.

Drilling is often seen as mindless repetition, and often, indeed, that's how people approach it. If they have a hundred facts to learn, they run through them, beginning with the first and going through to the last, until they know them all or (more likely) collapse or fall asleep or run out of time. But it needn't be that way. If you have a hundred facts on flash cards, you can go through them, beginning with the first, and going through to the last — once. As you do so, you can easily *set aside* the things you *do* know, and what's left is a reduced set of things you *don't* know. Go through that again. Continue doing this, pulling out the things you know and putting them aside (don't throw them away, but *get them out of your way*) until you have whittled the stack down either to nothing (which will take less time than you think) or until you have a very small stack on which you need to exercise other heavier tools. The ability to get the dross out of the way (in this case, what's already known, and therefore doesn't need to be studied) is the key to using one's time effectively to focus on the real problem (that is, what *isn't* already known, and so still needs to be conquered).

In this course, a large portion of the challenge facing many students is just getting two thousand years' worth of data into some kind of order. When you think about it that way, it should hardly come as a surprise that it's tough. It's a tall order. I have generally recommended that students make a deck of cards for themselves as the course progresses. Few follow the advice from the start, but those who do have profited thereby.

Here's how:

Start with an ordinary 3"x5" index card. Put the name of the work on one side (the unlined side is probably the best one for this). On the other (the lined side), indicate:

- the author, if known;
- the author's dates (approximate, if precise dates aren't known);
- the region and language in which the author was working;
- the major issues arising in class on this work — a few words should suffice for each.

That doesn't sound too hard, does it? *Every student should know each of these facts for every work we study — without exception.* Given that this means acquiring one to three such sets of facts per week, that's not a huge burden, if one takes it on as the course proceeds. If left to the end, though, it becomes quite a chore, and fosters that chronological fogginess in which one can refer to the eighth-century A.D. classical Greek poet Horace, or Christian saints writing in the year 450 B.C. It doesn't need to be that way.

Having made such cards, how does one make the best use of them? Well, there are three basic principles:

- Get the known out of the way. It's like food that's already been digested, and has no more nutritive value. We'll leave the analogy there.
- Use and create study time efficiently to maximize effectiveness.
- Review strategically.

We've already discussed the importance of the first of these. Practical methodologies for getting the known out of the way include having cards sorted into two stacks in front of you on a table or a desk, or having two jacket pockets into which to sort them as you go through them. Whatever works is fine. The point is to keep attacking the *unknown* material over and over — and to whittle it away till it's gone. Even one card eliminated from a deck on a pass is a local triumph: it's not only a positive gain of its own, but it also represents a diminution of the stack remaining to be conquered.

Second is making good opportunities for drill. Many very diligent students, aware that they are going to have to put an hour or more into the material per day, carve out an hour or an hour and a half all at one go, and sit down to give it their bravest effort. I admire their tenacity and industry — but they are working at a fraction of peak efficiency that way.

In fact, studies of learning patterns and psychology have turned up some rather interesting data. For *most* students, *most* of the time (there is no one-size-fits-all solution), it turns out that, no matter how long their study period may be, the most effective part of it is the first and last five to ten minutes. Assuming a younger student, let's be conservative and say five. Accordingly, if a student studies for an hour and a half at a go, he's really used ten minutes well. That's just a shade above a 10% return on time spent. No wonder it's disheartening. On the other hand, if a student only spends ten minutes, he's also used ten minutes well. That's a ninth the time spent, and 100% return on the investment.

An analogy may help. If you want to brew coffee, you can put whole beans into the basket and run the percolator all day — but the product will be pretty sad. To make a cup of coffee, you'd have to go at it for a long time, and use a lot of beans, at the end of which, you still probably wouldn't have done very well. Grind up those same beans, though, and you'll extract a lot more from them in much less time. Study is like that: break up study periods for this kind of thing (any-thing involving drill, at least) until it's all made up of the first and last five minutes, and you're going to achieve maximum "extraction". If a student does drill for no more than ten minutes at a time, with no fewer than thirty minutes between the sessions — but does them this way three times a day, for a total expenditure of half an hour (as needed), an astounding amount can be learned — much more than a half hour at one go. Once the process is well established, he or she probably won't be able to fill half an hour with it every day. There won't be anything left to go over.

What's more, these five- or ten-minute opportunities arise remarkably frequently, at times when one wouldn't expect to be able to study. A student can go through some drill cards while on the way to a piano lesson (though not while driving, please). One can go through a few while standing in line at the grocery store, or while waiting in the outer office for the dentist — it's better than six-month-old magazines. When dinner's going to be ready in ten minutes, one doesn't probably have time to read a significant piece of a book, but one *can* go through a few cards. In short, one can carve half an hour's worth of drill study out of in-between times that would otherwise be wasted throughout a day. At the end of the process, the study is done *and* the time that would have been devoted to this kind of study can be given over to something else. One can feel remarkably virtuous for accomplishing so much, at no real cost to oneself, while winding up with more free time into the bargain. It's a hard deal to beat.

The third ingredient is timely review. Once one has conquered a stack of cards, one should revisit it from time to time — for the first time after a few days, and then perhaps weekly thereafter. It shouldn't take long — most of the facts will be down cold, requiring a quick glance to give the assurance that they're still where they were when last seen. The handful of rebellious little facts that slip away can be rounded up like straying sheep and subdued before they become a problem.

I can virtually guarantee that any student who makes and uses cards as I've described through several five-to-ten-minute sessions daily, and then reviews them weekly, will have no trouble passing this course. I have set up the exam structure so that more than half of what is tested is objective factual material, and if that's nailed down, one can beat the 50% level. Really doing well is another matter, but at least passing will be virtually assured. What's more, the groundwork for the more difficult material will be in place, so that it can proceed much more effectively.

MEMORIZATION

A large portion of what we've just been talking about is memorization. Drilling is a matter of repetition, and as the Romans said, *repetitio mater memoriae.* That is, *repetition is the mother of memory.* But some bits are always hard to subdue, for no very clear reason. They take a different kind of work. I'd like to address this problem specifically, since I get e-mail from students (and their parents) with the all-too-common refrain, "I'm no good at memorizing things. I can understand concepts, but I'm no good at names and dates."

This may be true, but it's not just one of those things you have to accept, like colorblindness or the inability to leap a hundred feet into the air. Memorization, like almost any other human capacity, is a learned skill, and it can be taken vastly farther than most people ever suspect. Homeric bards could recite the *Iliad* from beginning to end. The Elder Seneca claimed (and there is no reason to doubt him) that in his youth he could hear a list of a hundred names once, and recite it back *verbatim* forward or backward. More convincing, perhaps, is the fact that even the student who cannot remember twenty key events of the *Iliad* or the *Nibelungenlied* will often have remarkably little difficulty remembering a hundred obscure details about "Star Wars"; the student who cannot connect each of the authors we read and discuss with his works can link ten times as many popular music artists with their hits. Why is that?

It's an odd fact of modern education that it has tended to dismiss memorization as somehow beneath us, rather than exploiting the things that have been learned about it for the past three thousand years, through the study of both classical rhetoric and cognitive psychology. Even granting that Seneca was a prodigiously talented speaker and master of the art of memory, still his techniques were practical, not magical, and of a sort that ordinary people can follow with surprising success. The key is so simple as to be obvious: *we best remember things that are connected with other things we already know.* This is just the way our minds work.

Accordingly, if you have a hundred facts to learn about, say, a period of history, it's going to be harder to learn the first dozen or so than all the rest of them put together. For the first, the mind has to construct a set of relations in a blank conceptual space without other reference points — but once learned, those first facts become anchor points for the rest, and the job gets easier.

What the ancient rhetoricians knew — and they made no secret of it — was that one could learn almost any arbitrary set of facts, including unrelated words, concepts, parts of a speech, *etc.*, by *forcing* the association with something arbitrary. There is not room here to develop this concept very extensively, but there are plenty of books out there, and most of them are built around the basics of a method at least 2500 years old. The books by Harry Lorayne or Kevin Trudeau will be helpful and useful to a student who believes he or she cannot learn to memorize things — but they contain nothing really new.

The following two examples are cases in point.

If you tell me, slowly, a list of twenty (or thirty, or forty) different words, as arbitrarily selected as you like, I can hear it once, and then can repeat it back to you, backwards or forwards. Am I a genius?

Hardly. I just know the trick.

I have taught it to students in a single ten-minute stretch of a class session. It's easy. One day about seventeen years ago I couldn't have done that to save my life. The next day I could — because I'd learned the trick. It's simple enough: for each word, one needs to form a mental picture representing that word (not necessarily a picture of the thing as such, if it's a thing — this will work as well with abstract concepts or verbs). Then as each new word comes along, one forms a mental "movie" connecting the image for one word to the image for the next. The more absurd and bizarre the image, and the more outrageous the connection between one and another, the better. It may take a few minutes' practice to learn to do this, but one can really master the technique in less than an hour, and when you are finished, you will be able to do this for any list you hear. If you hear it just once, but listen attentively and form the pictures, you will be able to remember the whole list. You'll forget it in a day or two, if you want to — but if you want to remember it, just run through it a few times every day for a few days, and then every few weeks, and it's yours for life. It's just that simple and that fast.

Of course memorizing lists of arbitrarily unrelated words is not the be-all and end-all of the educational process. But the fact that we can do so suggests that our memories merely need to be trained to be a lot more productive for us.

More useful perhaps is something like memorizing a speech. Ancient speakers, who had to speak without notes or teleprompters for an hour or two at a go, did it this way. They would envision a house they knew well — usually their own. They would have a particular path through the house, going from one room to another. In each room, they'd have five or ten items they'd touch or examine. With each item in each room, they'd associate one concept or idea in their speech. Once one has forged these links, recalling the entire speech in order is only a matter of mentally reconstructing one's walk through the house and imagining that one is touching each of the items in turn. One of course will still have to work on the finer points of phrasing — but that's not usually the hard part. The main points will not go missing, and they will all reliably come out in order.

This one still works too. Try it.

I offer neither of these as itself *the* solution to all the memorization one is going to need in school, but both of them are useful, and both of them will in fact produce some genuine benefits for you if you apply them. In less than five minutes, an average student, armed with a one-sentence summary of each of the books of the *Odyssey*, say, would be able to memorize what came in what book, and to repeat that list on demand to anyone who cared to ask. I've never asked anything that extensive of any of my students, but it would actually be a fairly trivial thing to achieve.

NOTE-TAKING AND LOG-EDITING

Practically speaking, taking notes on a text chat is neither necessary nor likely to be effective as a way of preserving data. A chat session can be logged, and preserved entire for future review, and there's nobody who could construct notes that quickly or that precisely. That's how our chat works.

This is a mixed blessing. There is certainly an obvious advantage about having a whole class log to review any time one wants to do so. There is one respect, however, in which not having to take notes may well be to the student's disadvantage. I discovered in high school and college that if I took notes in a class, I tended to do better. This in itself was not particularly surprising: what *did* surprise me, though, was that *it seemed not to matter much whether I actually ever looked at those notes again*. If I went over and *edited* the notes, it might help — but just reading through them was of fairly slight benefit.

What I eventually realized (and I later found that generations of other cleverer people had figured it out long before I did) was that the chief value of note-taking was not in *having* the data thus acquired in some sort of repository (usually books could be found containing all of the information and more); it was in *having worked with the data*. Doing something active, and especially being forced to put the ideas into my own words: those were the things that enabled me to get my mental hooks into the information.

In the introductory orientation sessions we have sometimes held at the beginning of the year, I have heard one student after another, when giving a presentation on how to be successful in these courses, say that one ought to *go through and edit one's logs*. There's really no mystery here: it's just as I have reported. The benefit is not to be found in the resulting document; the edited files could probably just as well be discarded upon completion (though few will want to). The benefit is in the *process*. Despite such enjoinders every year by our most successful students, only a small minority of new students apparently actually do this. They are, however, almost invariably among the top 10% of performers on exams. Draw your own conclusions from this fact.

ANALYSIS AND EXPLANATION

As one reduces, sifts, and otherwise handles the materials in the class discussions and in the readings through such things as writing notes, making charts, or editing logs, there are two results. One is the simple and fairly obvious consequence that the factual basics — the point of that first kind of study we were discussing above — become more familiar to the student. This is of course good. The other outcome, though, is that the student begins to think independently about the matter at hand, and to move into that second kind of study. That's even better.

In addition to drilling on facts and reorganizing notes or editing logs, probably the best way to acquire a really intimate familiarity with the material is to be forced to explain it to someone else. The Romans had another saying: *docendo discimus* — *we learn by teaching*. They were onto something. As soon as you have to teach something, all those dusty corners that didn't quite make sense are exposed. You are forced to confront your own ignorance. Very much as the cards did, it singles out and identifies those areas that were unclear. Organizing information in such a way as to be able to explain it clearly is useful not only to the recipient of that explanation, but also to the one doing the explaining. As someone who has taught algebra to my own children, after doing fairly poorly at it in high school, I can attest to the truth of this from my own experience. (I also came to *like* algebra a lot more into the bargain.)

You can help your student with this one in the simplest way — merely ask leading questions about what's going on, and insist on an explanation. Don't badger — but invite the explanation at dinner or on the way from here to there, and then probe anything that seems unclear or vague. Ultimately it will help; it will also probably create further channels for subsequent work. You might even learn some things you will find interesting, as well.

Essay-writing

The ultimate form of explanation is, of course, writing. That's an explanation for someone else and for oneself. Whereas reading makes a full man, as Francis Bacon says, and conversation a ready man, *writing makes an exact man*. It's a station to which we should all (irrespective of gender, which was not at issue at the time) aspire. There is no substitute for precision. It improves every field of study.

While most of the exams do have essay-answer sections, it's also the case that, with the volume of students we have, and the variety of levels at which they enter Scholars Online, there is no way to incorporate a great deal of writing into this course as such. This doesn't mean that students shouldn't be doing it: indeed, there is probably nothing that will more effectively exercise their analytic capacities and prepare them better for exams here and other written materials later on. Have your students write. Have them write for you. Have them write for each other. Have them work with one of the writing tutors. I have provided our writing program with a list of questions that can draw on material from this and every other literature course I teach (with the exception of my Senior English course, which itself entails a large amount of writing, which I grade and comment on myself). Do anything to get your kids writing at some level or another. It's probably the most important skill one can have in high school or college, and it remains useful afterward. If you have any doubts about this or about how writing issues can be approached or resolved, please get in touch with me. Often parents or students leave this one till it's too late to help out in this class — be more positively active: take the first step yourself. Insist that writing happen somewhere, and that the written products be accountable to some objective standards, both in quality of writing and of familiarity with the subject matter.

COURSE UNITS AND
WEEK-BY-WEEK LESSON GUIDE

The following is offered as a general overview of the course from the parents' perspective. It's not a substitute for the web-based curriculum outline, for which students are still answerable. But it's an explanation of what's going on, together with a bit of thematic material and an explanation of how each part contributes to the overall pedagogical goals I've outlined above. It's neither complete nor does it completely circumscribe the goals and processes, some of which emerge dynamically in the heat of discussion. But it should enable you to talk to your children somewhat more knowledgeably about the course (assuming you're not already following along and doing all the reading yourselves), and to ask those leading and probing questions I encouraged you in the last section to ask.

WEEK 1: INTRODUCTORY

In the first class of the year, I merely try to clarify how things work. Most of the time a fairly high percentage of the students are complete novices, and have no familiarity with our procedures beyond the mechanics they've learned from orientation classes. So I go over the course, review the basic rules of class protocol, and then let the students ask about anything that still seems foggy to them. It usually fills up the hour, but it's remarkably undirected — I want everyone to feel comfortable with the processes, so that we can get to the actual material itself.

Then, because not everyone comes to our class with the same degree of historical preparation, I give a quick summary of the major historical pathways we'll be treading in the coming nine months — from the world of the ancient Mediterranean, through the rise of Greek and Roman cultures, through the coming of Christianity, the breakup of the Mediterranean unity, down through to the fourteenth century. It's a whirlwind tour, and grossly inadequate, of course, but it helps to put up *some* signposts.

In addition to this, I try to get a few basic terms out on the table to talk about — among them *hero* (an ongoing theme of the course, as discussed above), and *myth*. We will be using the latter as it is used in history and anthropology, not as it is popularly used, and I want to make sure everyone understands the distinction. In our usage, the term *myth* refers to a story that conveys the core values of a culture and creates for people a sense of collective and individual identity within that culture. Please note that this definition says *nothing* about whether these myths are true. It doesn't say that they are (I will enthusiastically subscribe to the theory that the majority of them are not), but neither is it a dismissive term that means something like "a made-up story" or the like. This allows us to handle the central myths of the Jewish and Christian people (the Lord's covenant with Abraham, for example, and the death and resurrection of Christ) and the central myths of other peoples on common terms. That's not because they are interchangeable or because one is as good as another — I'm far from being a relativist. Rather it's because unless we *can* place them on a common footing, there is no way to compare them, and that comparison is important and useful.

Unit 1: The Hebrew Tradition

At the beginning, the Hebrew tradition is not a part of what we would consider the Western European culture, but its strands will at several different points feed into that overall picture, and so it seems a good idea to put down our roots here. Moreover, doing so allows us to move from material with which *most* of our students are reasonably familiar (this is certainly the most Biblically literate context in which I've taught), with some sense of security. It also will provide us the footing for later comparisons as we build the picture of who is doing what, what a hero looks like, and so on.

Week 2: The Foundation of the Jewish People

The key questions that come up in this first session are how the writer describes the characters in the narrative, and what we do and do not find out about them in the process. In particular, we focus on the story of Abraham.

One of the most important distinctions I have found it necessary to draw early in the course is the distinction between what is being shown in a particular piece of literature and how it is being shown. For some students it is an article of faith that the Bible is the best book of all, and so it shows us all the best things about the best people in the best way. I'm not going to argue against that position — but it substitutes an *evaluative* category for an *interpretive* one, and so it does not go very far toward the analysis of what really is going on. There are many things that the scriptural narratives do not tell us. The picture we are given of Abraham is in some ways quite brilliant, but in others it's very murky. One of my goals is to get the students to realize that this assessment is not in any way a condemnation of Genesis, but merely an observation of a fact that may actually tell us something positive about what the author was and was not concerned with. It's no slight to Genesis to say that the picture of Abraham is not itself one of the best character studies in all of literature — because that was apparently not the author's point in the first place. It's a rough passage for some students, but in the long run I think the benefit is worth the struggle.

This discussion also looks forward to the comparison we will eventually be drawing in week nine (using the first chapter of Auerbach's *Mimesis*) between how Abraham is shown and how Odysseus is shown.

> *Topical issues*: The hero; heroes of the faith and how they relate to our notions of heroism.

> *Pedagogical issues*: Figuring out what the author is really driving at; distinguishing the *what* of literature from the *how*.

WEEK 3: HEBREW POETICS AND THOUGHT

This week we take on the Psalms and Job, as well as casting a quick backward glance at the material from last week.

The first big theoretical literary question I throw at the students is simply this: *What is poetry?* When we start, almost everyone is quite confident about knowing what the term means. By the time we're finished, nobody is quite sure. Is this progress?

I think it is, because it causes us to question some hitherto unquestioned assumptions. The continuing student will revisit the issue throughout four years of study, up through Senior English, where we talk about the same question, but armed with a good deal more material from the intervening years. The difference in the level of discourse is remarkable.

One of the intriguing byproducts of the discussion is that it reveals some interesting facts about the unique nature of Hebrew poetry, and the reason why it, perhaps uniquely among the world's poetic material, is fairly well-suited to translation, whereas most poetry cannot really be translated with any kind of fidelity.

Topical issues: The hero, revisited. What is poetry?

Pedagogical issues: How do we talk about questions of definition, where there is no simple and agreed-upon definition? Can we use a term like "poetry" to mean one thing, without any further qualification? What are the limits of the process?

Unit 2: Greek Epic

Greek epic is represented here entirely by Homer (or the body of
poetry that travels under his name). In fact there were other Greek epics: the surviving Homeric poems (*Iliad, Odyssey*) are only two of what
was originally an epic cycle of several dozen lengthy poems (all lost,
save for some scraps and quotations), and there were also later forays
into the epic medium by such authors as Apollonius Rhodius. But
these two are among the linch-pins of western culture, defining as they
did major landmarks for the ancient world, both Greek and Roman,
and impressing themselves upon our culture with an immediacy that
is lacking in many of the later products. The date of their composition
(if they were even composed at a single time) is unclear; the Trojan War
itself seems to have taken place sometime around 1200 B.C. — give or
take a century or so — and there's some reason to think that the poems
were more or less in their current form by 800 B.C. or shortly afterward.

Week 4, Homer, *Iliad* 1

This week, we first attempt to get our feet on the ground with
Homer, to make sure that everyone is understanding him, what his
main terms are, and how he works. We talk about artistic conventions
such as the Homeric epithet and the nature of formulaic composition
(as far as can be discerned, the Homeric poems were put together
largely using formula-phrases). I attempt here and later in the sequence to explain how these formulae work.

I also attempt to put the narrative of the Trojan War into historical and literary context, so that students will be able to assess it for what it is. What we have is a historical and mythic narrative filtered through several layers of intervening cultural and literary history. What does that do for us?

> *Topical issues*: The hero in heroic-age Greece, and the issue of *kleos aphthiton*, or undying fame. How is the Homeric hero to be assessed on the terms of his own culture?

> *Pedagogical issues*: Achieving enough distance and objectivity to assess what kind of hero Achilles is; how to read a poetic survival from a very alien culture.

WEEK 5: HOMER, *ILIAD* 2

This week we continue discussing the nature of Homeric poetics and composition, and how epithets are used by the epic poet. We review the idea of the epithet a bit, and also briefly discuss the way in which poetic meter (in Greek, rhyme was a non-issue, but there was a very tightly constrained pattern of long and short syllables) helps shape composition.

From there, we go on to discuss the central matter of Book IX of the *Iliad*, which is to say, Why Achilles is Really Such a Big Deal. Much of my thinking about this issue has derived from the groundbreaking work of Gregory Nagy, related in his *The Best of the Achaeans*. It attempts to locate the nature of Achilles as a hero in the terms of his own culture. In particular, we discuss the relationship of the hero and the poet — the fact that neither the hero nor the poet is really complete without the other: the former because he has no one to spread his fame (*kleos*) and the latter because he has no one about whom to sing. How are these issues central to the embassy scenes in *Iliad* IX?

Finally, we also talk about what apparently makes characters act the way they do. What motivates them? How is motivation of characters represented in Homeric poetry? Many of the critical issues are given more than one completely compelling reason for coming about, often on different levels of the narrative (say, internal *vs.* external, or psychological *vs.* divine prompting). How are these related? What do they have to do with one another? Does such overdetermination reinforce or undermine a notion of cause and effect?

> *Topical issues*: The hero, in general; the mutually dependent relationship of the hero and the poet; *kleos* as the goal of both. Determination of action and character motivation, and how character motivation can be variously represented in a narrative.

> *Pedagogical issues*: In particular, how to zero in on the core values of an alien culture. What are our tools? How can we use vocabulary and word-usage to help us pry out of the poem what its basic terms are?

WEEK 6: HOMER, *ILIAD* 3

This week we wrap up Homer's *Iliad*. It's in some ways a kind of grab-bag of different kinds of discussion, but we try to cover each of them in some depth.

The nature of philological argument and reasoning is something that's close to my own roots as a classicist, and so first I try to explain a few things about it. One of the most fascinating facts about Homer — and it's difficult to explain without at least dipping into the Greek — is the fact that the language of Homeric poetry is actually an artificial language that grew up over many generations: no population at any point *ever* spoke the language that we now know as Homeric Greek. The poems themselves are like a slice through the stratified history of the language — almost a linguistic Grand Canyon.

Second, I try to provoke some discussion of the *ecphrasis* in *Iliad* XVIII, the description of the shield of Achilles. This is valuable for a number of reasons; first of all, it's an interesting device on its own, since it represents a complete halt in the forward movement of the narrative in order to describe a physical artifact at length. This will have immediate (if perhaps short-term) bearing on the similar arrested narrative of the latter part of the *Odyssey*, the passage dealing with the hero's scar, which is discussed brilliantly by Auerbach in his first chapter. It is also the first of at least half a dozen ecphrastic passages we'll be examining throughout the year to see how this technique is used, and to what effect.

Finally, we try to sum up the *Iliad* — what is its point? What's it really saying to and about us as human beings, and what does that have to do with the nature of humanity even today? Are the human lessons of the *Iliad* bounded by the confines and presuppositions of a pagan heroic-age culture? Or is there something we can extract from it for ourselves, as twenty-first century Christians?

> *Topical issues*: The hero as man, god, or animal, and how Homer's diction forces us to evaluate him differently; *ecphrasis* introduced. Philological reasoning.

> *Pedagogical issues*: How the concrete particulars of language and language usage are in fact valid fields of investigation, and can tell us a good deal about the substance of a given work. How to look for key terms and pry out their kernel of meaning.

WEEK 7: HOMER, *ODYSSEY* 1

The *Odyssey* is a shorter work than the *Iliad*, and so I encourage students to try to read it in two, rather than three weeks (though we will spend three weeks discussing it). This is largely so that they can tackle Auerbach's *Mimesis* in the third week without any further encumbrance: it's a tough new kind of reading for most students, though most have shown that they can handle it if they apply themselves. Some students won't quite be able to finish the *Odyssey* in two weeks, but that's not a disaster — we can make do.

One of the things that strikes almost everyone who has gone through both the *Iliad* and the *Odyssey* is just how different the two poems are — not just in narrative details, but in tone, and, eventually, in their views of the moral universe and life in general. Odysseus is a very different *kind* of hero from Achilles, and at a number of points in the poem the author (call him Homer if you like) seems to be taking jabs at the heroism of the *Iliad*. This distinction between the two poems not only helps distinguish the *Odyssey* from its predecessor; it also highlights some of the thematic issues of the *Odyssey*.

Odysseus, whose task is to get home after the war, through a grueling ten-year journey that takes him to a number of real and imaginary places, is more intrinsically self-sufficient than Achilles: he works with and for his men, but his story is quintessentially his own, and when his men are lost (as the poet puts it, they have lost their *nostos* — their homecoming) his story is still not over. He has a deeply rooted sense of self, and seems not to require the *kleos* that can be conferred by others. He values it, of course, but his chief goal is to reach home intact, and, once there, to rid his house of the parasitic suitors who are seeking the hand of his wife. This he accomplishes with resourcefulness and cunning. Whereas Achilles' mind is seldom hidden from us, it is often hard to tell exactly what Odysseus is thinking — but it's clear that the poet *values* thinking: there's an underlying brains-*vs.*-brawn theme running through the whole.

The *Odyssey* is admittedly an episodic work, and some have commented on this negatively; but while it lacks the single forward pressure one finds in the *Iliad*, its themes are interwoven with a subtlety and complexity virtually absent from the earlier poem. It seems superficially more like an adventure story than the *Iliad* does, but at the same time raises and re-raises thematic points, turning them over and reflecting on them in different contexts. Taken *in toto*, the poem is a very detailed survey of bronze-age Greek values pertaining to hospitality in particular; it also plays with meaning, storytelling and personal values.

People have also noticed how differently people, and especially women (human women and goddesses both) are handled in the *Odyssey*. This may go along with the brain-*vs.*-brawn question: certainly the women in the *Odyssey* are remarkably perceptive and subtly realized characters, ranging from Nausicaa, a charming and star-struck teenage girl who finds Odysseus on the shore, to the overbearing virago Circe (a witch whose hospitality includes turning her guests into swine) and from the enduringly faithful (but not untroubled) Penelope to the broken figure of the formerly adulterous Helen, holding forth in the Spartan court in a loveless and desperate household, and dulling her pain with drugs. But the male characters are also complex and occasionally beset with intriguing internal conflicts, and both Agamemnon and Achilles, whom Odysseus meets in his visit to the underworld, are embittered and full of regret. On the whole, the poem is shockingly modern and psychologically realistic in its views of people, but through all, it is also sympathetic and penetrating. The characters here are probably unparalleled in the rest of Greek literature.

> *Topical issues*: Questioning the Homeric hero: Odysseus as anti-Achillean hero; *kleos vs. nostos*. Brain *vs.* brawn and the gods' attitudes toward both. Narrative within a narrative. The problem of Homeric authorship.

> *Pedagogical issues*: The fact that differences in translation do *not* necessarily denote differences in the underlying text. How do we approach historical questions with literary ramifications, *e.g.*, the problem of Homeric authorship?

WEEK 8: HOMER, *ODYSSEY* 2

This week we try to finish up the narrative of the *Odyssey*, and so I first field questions about that, and try to establish what is going on, to whom, when, and so on. From there we move on to a variety of issues, some of them sensitive or problematic. What do we make of the fact that Odysseus is an accomplished liar? What do we make of the issue of his wife's faithfulness *vs.* his own nine-year (perhaps enforced but nevertheless unfaithful) dalliance with Calypso? Who are the Phaeacians, and what endows them with their strange and mystical existence?

Beyond this, there are lines linking the hero with Zeus and Metis — *metis* being a word meaning "craftiness" or "wiles" — but an almost cultic word, reserved, most of the time, for Zeus himself, and for Athena, his daughter by the personified Metis, who is Odysseus' constant guide throughout his homecoming and the purification of his house.

This poem is an almost inexhaustible nest of tangled themes, and we will of course not reach their limits, but the poem is a superlative example of how thematic material can be formed, permuted, and recalled through the use of particular vocabulary.

> *Topical issues*: The values of the hero. The themes of revenge; faithful *vs.* unfaithful wives; how the poem breaks down into sections or parts (along with some historical notes on the idea of *book*) and how they fit together.

> *Pedagogical issues*: More specifics about the translation format (prose *vs.* poetry). Looking at particular words as sources of

evidence for the thematics of the whole (especially *kleos/ nostos*, but also the vocabulary of guest-host relations, *etc.*

WEEK 9: HOMER, *ODYSSEY* 3

We spend our last week on Homer doing some cleanup discussion of the stray details of the poem, and then we turn to Erich Auerbach's magisterial *Mimesis*. The first chapter, "Odysseus' Scar", is largely a comparison of a passage of the *Odyssey* with a passage from Genesis, exploring how reality is represented in each text, and (implicitly) what kind of perceptual universe might give rise to that representation. *Mimesis* confuses some students at first, and offends a few: on a hasty or cavalier reading, it's possible to find Auerbach somewhat dismissive of Genesis.

I think he's in fact very far from being dismissive — but it's easy to misinterpret the fact that Auerbach recognizes that the voice with which Genesis speaks, and the claims it makes on its people, are simply beyond the scope of purely literary analysis, and this is not part of what he can reasonably address in a literary-scholarly mode. That much is surely correct. It eventually becomes quite clear, I think, that Auerbach has considerable sympathy with primitive Judaism and Christianity, and his literary judgments are both careful and penetrating, though they are scholarly, rather than devotional, in kind. Still, his reading of Gregory of Tours (Chapter IV, "Sicharius and Chramnesindus") should lay to rest any lingering apprehensions: it conveys with remarkable clarity the spiritual urgency that drives a sixth-century bishop, laboring among the barbarian Franks, to write, though he can't write very well; Auerbach also recognizes and appreciates his palpable love for his flock, despite their irrational and confusing ways.

We will cover the first seven chapters of *Mimesis* before the end of the year, but most of them fall in the second semester, because Auerbach was himself more a mediaevalist than a classicist. Here we use the book to get some fairly difficult ideas out on the table. Some students respond very well to his arguments — many telling me that in years afterward they continue to read him for their own edification. Others (among them some of my best students) find him bewildering from the start, and never really get him into their sights. Whatever happens in this regard, *don't worry about it*. I ask very few exam questions based on Auerbach. Those I do ask are typically given as one choice among several for an essay, and are usually based, as well, on points we've gone over in class. This is not a book one would normally assign to a high school class, and I know that — but I have found that some are able to appreciate what he's saying; and if so, why shouldn't they get the chance? The point here is that if your son or daughter gets something out of Auerbach, that's terrific. If not, it's not the end of the world, and maybe coming back to it in five or ten years will be better. Either way, it's okay.

If your student does have difficulty reading this chapter, but still really *wants* to get it, you have several options. One, of course, is reading it yourself and discussing it. I recommend that, because I think the book is remarkably illuminating; but it's also a good way of finding out how your student is thinking about these matters. If that gives rise to good conversation between you, all the better. If there are confusions that you think I could clarify, let me know. I'll be happy to help where I can.

Topical issues: The narrative of foreground and background, and again what we can learn about *what* the author wants to tell us from *how* the author is telling it.

Pedagogical issues: Reading past the surface of the work to understand how the composition of a narrative can represent a view of reality.

UNIT 3: GREEK TRAGEDY

Leaving Homer behind, we now leap ahead three hundred years or more to the Golden Age of Athens — that is, the fifth century B.C. The fifth century saw the rise and spread of Athenian democracy and with it a certain kind of civic leadership, the defeat of the Persians, an unparalleled explosion in the plastic and literary arts, the formation of vast trade alliances, and at the last the ruinous and suicidal Peloponnesian War, which brought devastation to much of Greece, but especially to the principal combatants, Athens and Sparta. Neither ever completely recovered, but Athens was more or less definitively crushed.

The greatness itself was genuine, though, while it lasted: the fifth century expressed a vision of the *polis*, the city-state, unique in the world up to that date. It was particularly at Athens that this reached its highest expression — a city small enough that more or less direct democracy was practical but large enough that when the city spoke as a single entity, it had some clout. At the beginning, democracy was seen in terms of a revelation, almost a gift from the gods, in terms that are strikingly similar to the passionate rhetoric of democracy one finds in the Age of Reason political philosophers from about 1750 to 1800.

In the midst of this, one of the clearest voices expressing the diverse (and often conflicting) hopes and fears of the people was Greek tragedy. Like most entertainment forms, it seldom speaks with an unambiguous or direct voice: but it speaks with gravity and a rich complexity that is hard to match. It is one of the great literary forms in the history of the world.

For all that, Greek tragedy is a grossly misunderstood form, and among those leading the misunderstanding are throngs of secondary

school teachers who have a few categories they relentlessly apply to
the one or two Greek plays they have read. By the end of this course,
your student will have read six (optionally nine) Greek tragedies, and
if he or she goes on to AP English, there will be three or four more
thrown in for good measure. Forget what you have heard about the
Tragic Flaw (supposedly at the core of every tragedy — but demon-
strably absent from most); forget as well what you've heard about *hu-
bris*, a term widely misunderstood to mean a Bad Attitude, but in fact
meaning nothing of the sort (it's actually more a transgression or an
outrage — in either case, an action rather than a state of mind). While
you're at it, forget, too, the notion that tragedies must end in calamity
or downfall. Some do, and some don't. Some are closer to what we'd
consider melodramas. Some of these categories are relevant to the in-
terpretation of *modern* plays constructed on the basis of these misunderstood ancient categories, but they do not apply very well at all to
the actual tragedies of the Greeks.

Many of these ideas are derived from the *Poetics* of Aristotle: but,
while it's true that he was indisputably a Greek, it should be noted
that:

• he was writing after the fact: all the great Greek tragedies come
from a time two to three generations before him;

• he never claimed to be writing a general pattern of all tragedy, but
to be describing the kind of tragedy he personally thought most successful;

• he was a far better logician and metaphysician than literary critic.

The point here is to take things as they come: the plays, which are
remarkably varied and express a wonderfully diverse perspective on
the world, will speak for themselves.

The origins of the drama, as your students will learn if they are doing their web reading, are very far back, and they lie not in an original attempt to *dramatize* anything as we understand the term, but rather in the medium of choral song arising from worship situations. Athenian tragedy came to be presented in the festival of Dionysus, the god of wine. What was once apparently something like a choral song acquired a soloist, and then that soloist began representing a particular character. With Aeschylus, one ran into multiple actors, who could then speak to each other — and when that happened, what that we would recognize as drama emerged.

The name *tragedy* means "goat-song" — surely one of the least useful and most perplexing etymologies ever to make itself known. The direct connection of most Greek tragedies to the substance of worship (with or without the involvement of goats) is quite perplexing from here; their connection with goats even more so. If it's any consolation, the contemporaries were equally perplexed: the phrase *ouden pros ton Dionyson* was coined apparently as a comment on the earliest of these plays: "Nothing to do with Dionysus." It's the articulate Athenian equivalent of, "Huh? What was *that* about?"

Nevertheless, the results have changed the world. We have only a handful of surviving dramas from only three Athenian tragedians: a remarkably small corpus. But in a sense, these plays are the great ancestors, for good or ill, of all subsequent drama in the western tradition — later Greek and Roman plays, mediaeval mystery and morality plays, the works of William Shakespeare, Pierre Corneille, Bernard Shaw, Henrik Ibsen, Anton Chekhov, Tennessee Williams, and George Lucas.

WEEK 10: AESCHYLUS

Aeschylus was the man who apparently first really saw the idea: one could move from a kind of concert setting with one solo actor to two (or more) and, in the process, go from something like a *recitativo* monologue to what was for the first time real drama, with characters interacting visibly in front of an audience.

Aeschylus wrote plays that are by any modern standards primitive. The moves are simplistic; the characters are flat and without any complexity of motivation and virtually no internal conflict; the development of the plot is often unclear. But his language was richly fertile, and overflowing with abstract ideas. His *Oresteia* is a trilogy comprising the *Agamemnon*, the *Choephoroi* (*Libation Bearers*), and the *Eumenides*; in the course of it he paints a grim picture of the old ways, and he becomes effectively the first artistic apologist for the new democratic order. He dramatizes, in a way that almost eclipses rational argument (unfortunately, perhaps), the way in which the old order, depending as it did on blood vengeance and infinite retribution — a "no-win" situation, in modern terms — could be addressed and vindicated by the institution of democracy and the jury trial.

Aeschylus himself was a serious man of action, certainly no stuffy aesthete. He was a veteran of the great wars that freed Athens and the rest of Greece from the Persian threat, and he considered that — not his monumental literary output — to be his most glorious claim to fame. But he saw in Athens a bright new hope — a new way of doing things. These plays at least (the authorship of the *Prometheus Bound* remains open to question, and the play presents some serious problems) give his vision of the state and the triumph of a rational, primarily masculine, sky-god principle which he expressed as Zeus, over an older, darker, primarily feminine principle associated with the earth, the earth-mother goddess, and blood sacrifice. The choruses of the *Oresteia* are saturated with such imagery, polarized into concrete opposites. Without some key to disentangle them, these references seem to be disjunct and arcane; with a key, however, they cohere beneath the surface. You may not always know quite why, but reading an Aeschylus play will not leave you unchanged.

> *Topical issues*: The tragic hero — is there such a thing? The chthonic vs. the uranic principles in mythic vocabulary. Triumphant vindication of democracy as well as the masculine principle (especially as embodied in Zeus).

> *Pedagogical issues*: Learning to read Aeschylean drama (it's not always easy to figure out how the choruses intersect with the dramatic action, for example).

WEEK 11: SOPHOCLES

Sophocles is in some ways the greatest of the Athenian tragedians — and at the same time one of the most treacherous to deal with. He was clearly Aristotle's favorite, and so many more of those categories we remember hearing about (and which I suggested you forget) actually *do* apply to Sophocles. Moreover, the *Oedipus Rex* (more properly *Oedipus Tyrannus*), is the one Greek tragedy most likely to have been read by anyone in high school. From it, all sorts of statistically unsound conclusions are drawn about Greek tragedy in general.

Be that as it may, the plays are great ones. They raise important issues that are still with us today, and treat them with mature grace. The two plays we concentrate on (*Oedipus Rex* and *Antigone*) address two issues of ongoing metaphysical and social concern: the first dealing with what to make of the idea of fate or destiny, and whether it is ever possible to avoid it, and the second with how one balances one's obligations to the society and state against one's obligations to one's religious convictions. Obviously, writing in the fifth century B.C., Sophocles' perspectives on both of these questions are untouched by Christian metaphysical or social thinking, but at the same time they are serious pieces of work, with a good deal to say to us even today.

In the class we also discuss some of the Aristotelian ideas that have been applied to these plays, and the notion of the so-called *dramatic unities* which were taken as guidelines for dramatists for many centuries. These dramatic unities chiefly have to do with continuity of time and space — the setting is unitary: that is, there are no "meanwhile, back at the agora" transitions, nor are there leaps forward (or backward) in time, as we have come to see in more recent dramatic products.

We also look at the *way* in which Oedipus is drawn, as opposed (chiefly) to Agamemnon and Orestes, and also to the figures in Homeric epic. With Oedipus we arrive at a new level of characterization in the drama, seeing for the first time his internal conflicts much more clearly than we ever saw those of Aeschylean characters.

Finally, we discuss also the issue of moral accountability that came up first in looking at Job, and in reference to the Old Testament Law.

What kind of accountability do we have for our actions if they are genuinely constrained by circumstance? To what degree are our actions ever really constrained by circumstance?

> *Topical issues*: Fate and predestination *vs.* moral accountability; responsibility to human and divine law; techniques of characterization. Dramatic, situational, and verbal irony.

> *Pedagogical issues*: Learning to look at a dramatic work for evidence of world-view; characterization as fundamental to story.

WEEK 12: EURIPIDES

The third of the Athenian tragedians has left us the largest surviving corpus — nineteen plays as opposed to seven each from Aeschylus and Sophocles — and they are remarkably diverse in their content and their expression of world-view and outlook. In the broadest terms, we can probably say that Euripides is the most pessimistic of the three: coming the latest, and writing many of his greatest works under the deepening shadow of the Peloponnesian War, his view of the state as an instrument of justice is far less rosy than that of Aeschylus; his view of the gods, likewise, is bleak and reflects a viewpoint in which humanity is little more than the plaything of divine caprice.

I have chosen one of Euripides' most famous plays — *The Bacchae* — and one of his least famous — the *Helen*. To say that either is characteristic of the author is impossible: in a sense the only way of typifying Euripides is to read everything he wrote (which also suggests that if another nineteen plays were miraculously to emerge from the sands of Egypt, we might have to revise our view of him entirely). The two do, however, represent a variety of ideas and points of view, and also present two very different tragic idioms.

The first is perhaps Euripides' clearest statement of what he sees as the moral chaos of the universe: it depicts Pentheus, a fairly conservative king of Thebes, who resists the introduction of the new cult of Dionysus into his city. He encounters a stranger, who is (as we know and he does not) Dionysus himself. Pentheus attempts to suppress the introduction of the cult, and at first simply fails; eventually he is entrapped, seduced by the prospect of viewing the forbidden rites (which involve a troop of frenzied women, the Bacchae or Maenads). He trespasses into their worship, and is torn apart (literally, but offstage) by the deluded Maenads, led by his own mother, who enters at the end of the play with his severed head, anciently represented by his mask, in her hands. Through it all, he is on the losing end of the deal, and it is not clear that any action he could have undertaken would have averted his grisly fate.

The *Helen*, by contrast, is at least superficially a sunny reinterpretation of the Trojan War myth: it presents the alternative story (already known in the time of Herodotus, who reports it as a possibility) that Helen never betrayed her husband Menelaus with Paris, but was instead swept off by the gods to Egypt, where she kept her virtue intact; the gods instead substituted a simulacrum (*eidolon*) of Helen to go off to Troy and get the Trojan War started — something they wanted for their own inscrutable purposes. The action of the play takes place when Menelaus, fresh from the victory after ten years at Troy, and one of the greatest stuffed shirts in all Greek literature, is blown off course and arrives in Egypt himself. The simulacrum, whom he had taken from Troy, disappears at this point, and Menelaus is reunited with Helen. There ensues a melodramatic plot twist in which they must escape the evil designs of the new Egyptian king, who wants Helen for his own. Through some quick thinking by the wily and virtuous Helen (who can outthink Menelaus in every possible way) they escape, and live, presumably, happily ever after. The subtext of the play, of course, is considerably darker than would appear on the surface, since the Trojan War turns out to have been fought for no reason: it suggests once again that the people are no more than the playthings of the gods, and are hence powerless to avert any of the calamities that beset them. They may, however, be able to preserve their own moral integrity — which is seen as a good thing on its own terms.

> *Topical issues*: The anti-hero; feminist reinterpretation of classical myths; moral accountability (again) and the designs of the gods.

> *Pedagogical issues*: Interpreting dramatic texts and subtexts for world-view ideas, and also seeing how an artistic voice can represent the loss of faith in cultural and religious constants.

Unit 4: Greek Philosophy and History

Because this is not a philosophy course, or even a generic "great books" course, we cannot get as involved in these authors as deeply as we might otherwise like to do. What they are doing here is not primarily literary in its intent, but they enter the literary mainstream of their times, ask vitally important questions, and do so with an extraordinary depth of thought. What's more, they write the results in truly marvelous prose.

Week 13: Herodotus and Thucydides

These two great historians of the Greek tradition represent distinctly different approaches to the historical enterprise, and give us a chance to think about what an historian does. Herodotus is writing from outside Athens in an Ionic dialect of Greek, about broad historical questions ultimately relating to the wars with Persia, while peppering his narrative with intriguing tales from all over — engaging in their own right, but moving only indirectly toward their final goal. Thucydides, on the other hand, is writing as an Athenian himself embroiled in the particulars of the Peloponnesian War; his steely narrative and gritty representation of the practical and moral horrors of war are as timely today as ever.

Both offer challenges for the reader, and both force us to question how history is — or ought to be — written. Herodotus unrolls his stories in a leisurely and discursive way, and often presents a variety of possible explanations for any given event. Which of them is true, he often declines to decide; just as often when he does express an opinion, his judgment is clearly absurd (as where he dismisses as ludicrous the notion that the sources of the Nile are in the melting snows of mountains to the south of Egypt). He has widely been called the Father of History; it's worth observing the relationship of what we consider history and the simple demands of story, which are both (etymologically) from the same root. He dabbles in anthropology, spending whole books telling odd details about the cultures of the Egyptians and Scythians; he also recounts with moving patriotic fervor such narratives as that of the Spartans at Thermopylae, who sacrificed themselves to a man, in order to delay the Persian advance and so give the remainder of Greece a fighting chance (which, as it emerged, ultimately saved the larger cause).

Thucydides, on the other hand, claims to be telling what happened, without adornment or embellishment as an inheritance for posterity (the Greek term is *ktema es aei*, but it may also be worthwhile to consider it as a latter-day reinterpretation of that *kleos* we first met with Homer); at the same time, he freely admits making up the speeches with which he shapes his arguments between the various principal forces. How is what he is doing different from the writings of Herodotus (whom he generally disparages)?

In hindsight, these two authors seem to have more in common with each other than either has with modern historians. Certainly both seem to view history as a kind of expression of moral philosophy, and an arena in which to argue moral issues. The good and bad choices we make shape our future; the character of the principal players sets in motion the destinies of nations and peoples. Ancient historiography never abandons this idea: we will see it again when we visit the Roman historians, and when we read Dante as well.

Topical issues: History and the story; fabricating historical matter for dramatic purposes; history as a moral enterprise and character as destiny.

Pedagogical issues: Determining what presuppositions we bring to different kinds of reading. What do we expect of history, as opposed to what we expect of other literary forms, such as epic or drama?

WEEK 14: SOCRATES AND PLATO

It has been said that the history of Western philosophy is in effect a series of footnotes to Plato. This is a reductive view, and, like all reductive views, at least partly wrong. But it is also partly right. Since the death of Socrates, western philosophy *has* been colored largely by what this remarkable man, whom many have compared with Jesus, thought and taught.

Of course Socrates was not the Son of God, and he had no redemptive notion of his own mission. He was an infinitely curious man on an intellectual quest, and his basic question was, "What is it?" But his approach is characterized by a few important hallmarks, and it is useful to confront those.

First of all, he was not as concerned as were his predecessors (meaningfully labeled, as an afterthought, as the Presocratics) with how the physical world was made up; he was more concerned with the makeup of the moral and metaphysical universe. He was primarily concerned with what was *good,* and he expressed an unwavering faith in *to kalon* — The Good — in everything he did. He was an annoyingly implacable foe to the trivial or superficial; he always managed to ask the question that most exposed the mental or moral bankruptcy of his interlocutors, and he wanted to know why it was good or right that anything should be as it was.

His moral teachings are simple and can be summed up with his own permutation of the Golden Rule — *mallon adikeisthai e adikein* — *it is better to be wronged than to do wrong.* He seems to have followed this conviction throughout most of his life, and to have followed it even to his death, which came about in the somewhat paranoid social and political climate at Athens in the aftermath of the Peloponnesian War.

He believed in the immortality of the soul, and that all people are in relation to a unitary higher power, from whom all creation comes. In these regards he seems, in flashes and glimmers, to foreshadow some of the notions of Christian thought. He is not, of course, Christian, and he does have other notions that cannot be squared with Christianity at all; at the same time, he represents the attempt — imperfect as it may be — of the natural man to achieve moral goodness.

His methodology has become famous and (typically) is often least understood by those who claim most loudly to be following it. He asked questions, leading others into an awareness of their own ignorance. He did this, apparently, out of a fixed conviction that truth could, at least in part, be discovered by the application of intellect, through the exercise of *dialectic* — which is, in a nutshell, nothing more than conversation (*dialegesthai*), with an emphasis on the give and take. He was accordingly a foe of the Sophists, whose program was rhetoric:

the ability of the speaker to persuade people to do the speaker's will, rather than their education to determine what the right thing is.

Many people have taken the "Socratic method" to denote a programmed series of questions and answers whereby the student is led — one might say dragged — into arriving at a predetermined set of positions that the questioner/teacher had in mind all along. This bears a certain superficial resemblance to Socrates' own methods, but it almost completely belies his intentions. Socrates tended not to ask about things he thought he knew: most of the time he seems to be asking about what he genuinely wants to understand. When one can extract a doctrinal burden from his argument, it is almost invariably of a negative sort — leading the student not to a fixed set of conclusions — or any set of conclusions — but to an admission of his own ignorance. This state, called *aporia* — the Greek (etymologically connected to our word "pore") means something like "being stuck" or "having no way through" — is where most of the early dialogues end.

The practical difficulty of getting at the words and ideas of Socrates lies in the simple fact that he never wrote anything. Almost all the Socratic material we have is related by Plato — who claims to be reporting Socrates' conversations, but since some of these conversations, if they happened at all, took place before Plato's birth, we have to be skeptical: certainly he was not an eyewitness, and he may be doing something similar to what Thucydides has done in terms of his speeches. This so-called *Socratic problem* is an interpretive stumbling-stone of sorts, but has (fortunately) not robbed the Dialogues of Plato of their power to challenge us.

We have three pieces of Plato this week — all of them very different. The first is the *Apology of Socrates*, which is Plato's account of Socrates' defense speech before the Athenian court, when he has been brought up on charges of corrupting the youth of the city. It expresses his view of what his own mission is, and his conviction about what he has to say. The second is the so-called "Allegory of the Cave" section from the *Republic* — a fairly short bit that relates, in an allegory of a man reared in a shadowy cave and then released to see the outside world and the sun, his own belief in a transcendent reality far beyond what we experience here on day-to-day basis, and also the difficulties confronting one who claims to know anything about that outside world. The final piece is his dialogue *Meno*, which lays out his doctrine of *anamnesis*, or recollection, which argues that whatever we know, we know from an earlier pre-existence in which we had more direct access to the divine. As an argument I personally think it's defective, but notions of this sort have very thoroughly permeated later thought, both Christian and pagan, and its terms deserve to be understood.

> *Topical issues*: The heroism of the martyr and philosopher; standing up for what you believe in. The nature of human knowledge; the question, again, of moral accountability.

> *Pedagogical issues*: How to read philosophical prose, how to use and how to understand the dialogue form both dramatically and as an exposition of positions. The importance of dialectic as a process.

Unit 5: Republican Rome

We draw the curtain on Greek culture, for the main part, in the middle of the fourth century B.C. This is a matter of convenience and time management for the course, not an intrinsic endpoint in the material. Greek-speaking culture continues for a number of years in Greece and most of the eastern half of the Mediterranean; it produces the culture generally called Hellenistic (as opposed to the Hellenic culture of the fifth century and before), and of which Rome itself is in many ways an heir. Vergil is writing as much in the tradition of Apollonius of Rhodes as of Homer, though I certainly believe that the work is more directly in *response* to Homer than to Apollonius.

Rome is a different story. By the time we pick up her literary products in the first century B.C., she has become a world power — extending political sway over almost all the Mediterranean and on the verge of controlling Europe to the Rhine and the Danube. Rome's problems are the problems of world empires, and of large, and largely idle, urban masses. While not as capriciously democratic in form as the Athenian state at its height (where almost any action could be proposed, approved, and executed, provided only that one got sufficient votes), the Republic presents us with some familiar dilemmas as timely as the last election. It's a culture in which the reins are held by a very few enormously powerful (and enormously wealthy) men, but in which that power still, at a critical point, passes through the hands of an electorate. It brings about a perpetual propaganda war waged upon the many in order to secure political support. In short, some of the patterns of Roman culture seem shockingly familiar today.

WEEK 15: CAESAR, CICERO, AND POLYBIUS

In order to ease the jump from Athens in the fourth century B.C. to the latter end of the Roman Republic in the first, I attempt to provide at this point some of the historical framework that will be necessary for what is to follow. We talk about that briefly to make sure that everyone is on the proverbial same page.

The readings themselves have been selected partly to allow students to take in the massive shift in cultural paradigms. We read three works of more historical than properly literary significance, but Cicero and Caesar were nevertheless among the greatest prose authors of the Roman republic, and their expressions of their own perspectives is itself intriguing. In addition, they lay much of the groundwork for what we'll be seeing later in Vergil's *Aeneid*. Polybius was a Greek author, writing in Greek, but about Rome.

> *Topical issues*: Caesar as self-aggrandizing hero and as propagandistic writer; modes of self-presentation for persuasion and propagandistic purposes; the personal goals of the strong man of the later Republic.

> *Pedagogical issues*: Further reading for clues about how the author is presenting himself; discerning narrative voice and tone in writing; distinguishing apparent purpose from actual purpose.

WEEK 16: LUCRETIUS AND CATULLUS

This week we have two radically different Roman poets. It would certainly be useful, had we the time, to devote separate sections to the two of them. Unfortunately, we are not able to fit in everything one might like to do as it is.

Lucretius was writing during the first century B.C., during the last century of the Republic. His purpose is didactic, and his poetry is, as is most ancient didactic poetry, in dactylic hexameter — that is, the epic meter. What cannot be shown or appreciated in a course like this is the richness of his Latin: he wrote in an archaizing Latin filled with old words and odd ending-forms, but with a musicality almost unmatched in his time. His purpose is to persuade his readers (and, I have always thought, himself) of the truth of the Epicurean philosophical world-view. Epicureanism is materialistic: it holds that nothing exists aside from matter (which is atomic) and void (in which the atoms move). Therefore, he argues, all concern for the gods and religion is wasted time, and inclined to lead us not only into error but into evil. The highest good in the Epicurean system is the avoidance of pain, and so Lucretius enjoins a life of restrained gentility, unencumbered by religion or strong passions. Religion, he argues (in one of the most famous passages of all Latin literature) is responsible for every kind of human degradation, a point he illustrates with a chilling (and ironically passionate) retelling of the story of Agamemnon's sacrifice of his daughter Iphigenia.

I am not of course trying to persuade anyone here to become a materialist, nor do I think that Lucretius' arguments are persuasive. But his poem is remarkable in a number of ways. First of all, it represents another use for a form we have come to regard as epic. Second, it is a very different kind of writing from what we will see in the rest of the late Republican Latin poets. Third, his story (especially the above-mentioned scene) vividly illustrates the endurance and the penetration of the Trojan War stories in the intellectual and social fabric of the ancient world. Here, in Rome, probably a thousand years after the events of the Trojan War, and seven hundred years after the composition of the Homeric epics, the events of that conflict are still the common currency of discourse — this is still the ultimate story from which a poet might be expected to draw examples.

Catullus, writing lyric poetry in the late Republic, differs in almost every way from Lucretius. He was one of the hip and with-it generation of poets generally known as the *neoteroi*, "the younger set" — sometimes called the neoteric poets. His diction is untouched by archaism; his philosophical stance is not a pressing issue: he mostly wants to have his girlfriend back. And yet in a few different places he too, dips into a different mode of discourse. And when he (apparently) sets out to write an *epyllion*, the product is characteristically a range of epic implication compressed into a single scene — the wedding-feast of Peleus and Thetis. They will be the parents of Achilles, and hence Catullus is invoking the Trojan War mythos by reference. The poem is also adorned with a very large ecphrasis (about half its 400 lines), which deserves attention as a case study in the next stage of the use of the form.

For these poets, I have had recourse to web publication. I've used a public-domain version of the *De rerum natura* of Lucretius. It's a bit old and stodgy and rather florid: in that respect, it's not unlike the poem itself. The Catullus poems are given in an assortment of translations. Those seeking print editions for either of these authors will find options in the bibliography. There are several good translations of the Lucretius available; I should, however, warn you that if you acquire a complete Catullus, it will certainly contain some material that many will find objectionable.

> *Topical issues*: The poet as spokesman for a position; conflicts within his own perspective. Persuasive writing (continuing from Cicero, Caesar, *etc.*) and its proper place. *Epyllion* and *ecphrasis* in Catullus; how *ecphrasis* can be used thematically as well as ornamentally. Introduction to the problem of epic composition looking forward to Vergil.

> *Pedagogical issues*: How to take apparently disingenuous statements from an author: irony and conflict of purpose.

UNIT 6: AUGUSTAN ROME

The Republic had begun to totter under the weight of an imperial administration: governing territories so widely dispersed became increasingly difficult without a strong centralized government, and the republican forms, which had served so admirably for a city (as Polybius attested) were over-burdened. Increasingly, the chief tool of policy was military force, and those who controlled the military became, *ipso facto*, the makers of policy. Into this picture entered political strongmen like Marius and Sulla (ca. 100 B.C.), who had risen through military command; their civil wars nearly tore Rome in half, and left many Romans dead under proscriptions and other systematic purges. A generation later, there arose, largely by the same means, C. Julius Caesar (elected consul and then made proconsul of Gaul, where he amassed incalculable fortunes through conquest), M. Licinius Crassus (an entrepreneur who is reputed to have invented the first fire company — quite emphatically for profit), and Pompey the Great, who managed to earn, early in his career, the nickname *adulescens carnifex* — "the young butcher": not a compliment then any more than now. For all of them, there were no limits to personal aspiration: Caesar overtly compared himself to Alexander and to Achilles; only dominion and a kind of reinvented Homeric *kleos* were of enduring value. Crassus had armies that he had bought and paid for; Caesar took armies raised by levy of Rome and made them his own through battle and plunder. Rome eventually came to civil war, and Caesar defeated Pompey and the Senate, and was established as dictator for life.

The office of dictator, despite modern usage of the term, was fully consistent with the republican constitution. In times of extreme crisis, a dictator could be elected or appointed to address the situation as a pair of consuls (the normal leaders of the state) might not be able to do. But the dictator's term was strictly limited to six months. Caesar received the power in perpetuity.

Not surprisingly, this offended a number of old-school republicans — even those who had fought on Caesar's side in the wars against Pompey. In 44 B.C., Caesar was assassinated, thus initiating another round of civil war. At the end of the process, all the chief conspirators were dead; but so were many of those on Caesar's side. M. Antonius, who had initially made common cause with Caesar's nephew and adopted son Octavian, used his powers as part of the so-called Second Triumvirate to eliminate many of his enemies, including the ultimate spokesman for the republic and the *concordia omnium bonorum* (*the alliance of all good people*), M. Tullius Cicero. But Antony soon got in Octavian's way and was eliminated in his turn, being defeated at the legendary battle of Actium. Octavian emerged from the fracas as the sole leader, and he imposed a sort of peace. He laid claim to the novel title *princeps* — often translated as "first citizen", but also (be it noted) the root of our modern "prince". He obtained, almost surreptitiously, the *tribunicia potestas* — the power of the tribunes, which gave him the veto power over virtually everything — from year to year. Officially, however, he held no regular office most of the time, and so claimed to be restoring the Republic. In reality, of course, it didn't matter a great deal what offices he did or did not hold — he had the pragmatic power and was well-schooled in exercising it.

In fact this is the beginning of what we now consider the period of the Empire; the Republic had died with Caesar, and was never to be restored in fact, whatever of the old nomenclature endured. But its forms and offices were kept in play for many generations, and it was a convenient fiction, at least, for those in power to be able to claim that the Republic was still the institution it had always been, and that the people were still in a sense the rulers of the state. Octavian (eventually awarded the title Augustus by the senate — the name by which he is principally known today) himself established this program carefully and very deliberately: he implemented the most sweeping changes ever to affect the Roman world under the guise of rebuilding the Republic. In the process, he sought to heighten the awareness of traditional values, and he wanted an official spokesman — one who would speak in traditional tones — for his agenda.

WEEK 17: VERGIL 1

That spokesman — at least by design — was the most capable poet ever to write in the Latin language, P. Vergilius Maro. (Yes, the spelling *Vergil* is preferred to *Virgil*, on etymological grounds: the Latin name is unambiguously *Vergilius*, but both *Virgil* and *Vergil* are seen quite often. In citing other sources, I have retained the spelling used in the source itself, but my own spelling is *Vergil*.)

Vergil (along with Catullus and Horace) was one of the so-called *neoteric poets* who had abjured the writing of epic or other long forms of poetry. It was not just a passive association, a kind of gang of poets he otherwise ran around with: there was a rather well-articulated vision of "poetical correctness" associated with the *neoteroi*, based ultimately on the ideals of the Hellenistic Greek poet Callimachus. Vergil

had himself been asked to write an epic, and he had emphatically de-
nied that he would ever do so. He wrote small, refined poems — pas-
toral poems about the loves of shepherds, and agricultural poems
about how to be a farmer and keep bees. Then he produced the *Aeneid*.
What are we to make of that fact? How can we square the denial with
the deed?

That question itself needs to inform how anyone thinks about the
Aeneid. The poem itself is a gigantic piece of work — not merely in size
(though it is twelve books of nearly a thousand lines each), but because
it was written with the kind of care for every word and every line that
the lyric poet typically lavishes on a twelve-line gem. It's minutely
crafted — certainly not pieced together out of epic formulae and narrative structures like the *aristeia* as was (apparently) the *Iliad*. It replaces
the stark Homeric realism with a subjective surrealism that is hard to
define, but remains inescapable at every turn. What is brilliantly illu-
minated in Homer becomes oddly cloudy in Vergil. Homer's overde-
termined action becomes underdetermined: sometimes we don't really
know *why* someone is doing what he's doing. What's more, it's con-
scious of its ancestry: it reflects the *Iliad* and the *Odyssey* at every stage,
in every few lines, as well as in its overall construction. What it means,
therefore, *cannot* be elicited directly even from the most attentive reading of the poem itself. One has to have read (and understood) Homer
to make sense out of Vergil.

Wendell Clausen, one of the great Vergil scholars of our day, has
said that the two best commentaries ever written about the *Aeneid* were
those written by Homer, and he's absolutely right. Obviously Homer
(whoever he was, or they were), composing his epics in approximately
750 B.C., knew nothing of Vergil, and produced no real commentary on

the *Aeneid*. At the same time, the *Aeneid* is from beginning to end a re-interpretation and a reassessment of Homeric terms and values. It asks about *kleos* again — through eyes that have seen the ruin of the Repub-lic by those who were grasping for it, here and now. It sets *kleos* and *nostos* once again up as foils, but makes the new homecoming an arri-val in a place that has not been seen before. All this seems to reflect the programs of Augustus, who proclaims a return to the traditional forms of the Roman republic, and yet refashions it entirely. How much is Vergil writing an epic, then — and how much is he producing an epic-length demonstration that epic is now impossible? Everything about the *Aeneid* is in some sense an inversion or eversion of Homer. The *Iliad* begins in rage — and that's where the *Aeneid* ends. It offers shadowy promises, including an apparently prophetic trip to the underworld, and then snatches the promises away by undercutting itself. Here is an epic that is, like the Callimachean *epyllion*, not an epic at all. At every turn it warns, "You can't go home again."

For this first week, we start to look at some of the parallels between the *Aeneid* and the Homeric poems, and we try to evaluate what those parallels disclose. We also look at the artistic integrity of the work as a whole, and how its local realism can in places undermine the realism of the whole. We also talk about Vergil's sequence of different kinds of *ecphrasis* along the way. I leave it up to the students to determine the meaning of the underworld visit with which Bk. VI closes. Why does Aeneas exit as he does?

> *Topical issues*: Rethinking the hero; *kleos, nostos,* and the ques-tion of a return for Rome. Can a literary form subvert not only a political program, but also itself? Is the *Aeneid* the

propaganda piece for the Roman empire? Or is it something else? Is Vergil just incapable of invention? Why are there so many parallels?

Pedagogical issues: Reading past the surface for a secondary or hidden meaning. Is the *Aeneid* a subversive piece of literature? What do we mean by that?

WEEK 18: VERGIL 2

This week we try to pick up on the issues we left hanging last time — how the conditional promises at the end of Bk. VI may or may not constitute real promises, and Vergil's darker vision of what he's doing. I also try to tie this in as possible with an overview of the history of the period through which Vergil himself had had to live; now we tie it in with our knowledge of how the poem ends.

Topical issues: The hero or the anti-hero?

Pedagogical issues: Much as last week.

[WEEK 19: TIME OUT; REVIEW FOR MIDTERM]

This class is largely run by the students: I'm open for suggestions and opinions, as well as questions. Bring issues, raise things that challenge or puzzle.

WEEK 20: HORACE

Because the principal midterm tends to overlap with the reading time for this week, I have kept the reading load to a minimum: the students are expected to read a few short poems by the Roman poet Horace. Horace was a friend of Vergil's: they both had the same prodigiously wealthy and influential patron named Maecenas, which put them on the edge of Augustus' inner circle. Whereas Vergil came from a family of gentleman farmers, however, Horace was the son of a freedman (that is, a former slave). It is a sign of the remarkable social mobility at Rome that someone from such humble origins could rise so far.

The poetic development of Vergil and Horace was similar, up to the point where Vergil wrote what seemed to be an epic. Both were adherents of the Callimachean school of poetry that considered epic as something repugnant; both strove to produce small and perfectly polished verbal constructions. Horace was also asked to write epic, apparently; but he declined in an elegantly-turned poem of the form that came to be known as *recusatio*. For the most part, Horace confined himself to lyric poetry and the occasional satire and verse epistle. His lyric poetry is collected in the four books of *Odes* and a short early collection called the *Epodes*: it is intensely disciplined, and at its best, of a crystalline compression and focus. Some of this emerges through translation, but we are concentrating this week on trying to see past some of those boundaries. For most of the poems, I have provided multiple translations on the website, in order to clarify the nature of the translator's task. It has always been interesting to watch students wrestle with this problem — most assume at the outset that there is a single obvious and correct way to translate anything, admitting at most only slight variation. Few have considered the possibility that a full translation may be effectively impossible; fewer still have considered the possibility that very different translations may capture different facets of a text.

Again, we are of course familiarizing the students with some great literature for its own sake, and I like (while letting the students choose several poems to discuss) to go over *Epodes* VII and *Odes* I.3 in particular. The former (*Quo, quo, scelesti, ruitis?*) is a brilliant and passionate youthful poem decrying the slide back into civil war. I know no better text in which to illustrate the effect of changing poetic address midstream: this will prove useful further in this course and also in English Literature, where we discuss something similar with Browning, as well as more general discussions of narrative voice in Chaucer. The latter (*Sic te diva potens Cypri*) is a so-called *propempticon* (a bon-voyage poem) addressed to Vergil on the occasion of his departure for Greece. The fact that Vergil is not known to have taken any trip to Greece contemporary with the writing of this poem is only one of the fascinating contradictions in the historical puzzle. The poem also takes on an apparent moralizing posture that is curiously ambivalent; this leads us into a discussion of how to understand such things. Should they to be taken at face value? What is the function of irony here? Is it possible that in writing the poem even Horace himself did not know what the desired outcome would be?

> *Topical issues*: Translation, and a good close look at a couple of these poems (explained) in Latin; the slippery nature of an overt message in a work of literature.

Pedagogical issues: Appreciating the problem of translating from a foreign language, especially poetry, and reading for non-obvious meanings.

WEEK 21: OVID

Ovid was one of the greatest technicians of Roman poetry; he produced an abundance of extremely fluent verse, with a masterly array of coloration and nuance. His love poetry (which we ignore almost completely) ranges from the racy to the mildly tedious; but his *magnum opus* is probably his enormous hexametric poem (*i.e.*, in epic meter) the *Metamorphoses* (not to be confused with the work of the same title — also sometimes called *The Golden Ass* — of Lucius Apuleius: in many ways a better work, but not entirely appropriate to this context). Ovid's *Metamorphoses* in fact is one of the leading sources of information about Greek and Roman myth; it may somewhat bias our view of those myths, too, inasmuch as it has as its central theme the divine transformation of one thing into another. Accordingly we probably have more stories of people being turned into trees (or stars, rocks, or small animals) than were really current in their own day. The *Metamorphoses* is an enormous work, though, containing a lot of stories.

The only real difficulty with it is that nobody yet seems to know what it's about (other than the obvious issue of things changing). It has defied thematic classification and analysis for two thousand years, and recently scholars are finally daring to admit the fact openly (*cf.* Joseph Solodow's volume on the subject). Normally, it would be a simple matter to determine that a multi-book hexametric poem on mythological topics ought to be regarded as an epic. Not so this one. Nor can it be considered didactic poetry.

We concentrate in class on one story — the tale of Phaeton, the son of the Sun-god (not explicitly Apollo here), who demands to be allowed to drive the chariot of the Sun across the sky, with predictably disastrous effects. Here we mostly focus on technique: how Ovid goes about telling his story, and what he shows us. In particular, too, I try to call attention to the splendid (though perplexing) instance of *ecphrasis* that occurs on the doors of the Sun's temple-palace. As with most of the rest of the poem, the question seems to be, "Okay, so what is it for?" It's a challenging piece of reading, but it can be useful as a point of comparison for other things, both earlier and later.

> *Topical issues*: The problem of Ovid's writing: his lack of a narrative focal point, his apparently deliberate avoidance of anything resembling thematic cohesion, and his way of pointing this out through his use of *ecphrasis*.
>
> *Pedagogical issues*: Figuring out what the author is really driving at; distinguishing the *what* of literature from the *how*.

WEEK 22: LIVY

There really is no convenient point at which to insert Livy into the lineup. He is not from Rome, but he writes of things Roman with the rare passion of the naturalized citizen or the convert. He is writing in the Augustan principate, but he reflects (in general) values of an earlier age. In his historical writing he is producing the kind of value-based narrative Augustus was probably looking to find in his much-requested epic.

Livy's enormous history of Rome originally took in everything from the earliest days down to Livy's own time, but only a small percentage of it survives (still the surviving part runs to many books). What remains is in several discontinuous chunks. The first deals with the legendary past, from the founding of Rome through the expulsion of the kings and the first clashes with the other Latin tribes; then there is another chunk dealing with the Punic Wars (especially the Second Punic, or Hannibalic War), and finally some more dealing with other wars around the Mediterranean, most particularly the Macedonian Wars of the second century B.C.

With Livy we re-open a number of issues: he illumines clearly the early Roman ideal of heroism and self-sacrifice for the good of the state and the community — an ideal that had been all but lost by the last century of the Roman republic, with leaders like Marius, Sulla, Caesar, and Pompey. (Cicero was arguably an adherent to these older beliefs, but he was never able to win over a large following.) Livy's heroic ideals throw different light on the later Roman models of heroism, and will, I hope, help clarify (if after the fact) some of the complex questions Vergil was asking.

At the same time, Livy was far from simple: in his own way, his history is as fraught with a social and ethical agenda as those of Herodotus and Thucydides, and his own rhetorical skills are quite considerable. He writes dramatic (though, from the point of view of classical Latin, somewhat non-standard) prose that's arresting, while manipulating the doubt and certainty of his readers with remarkable subtlety and sophistication.

Topical issues: The hero, especially the early Roman model, as compared with Homeric and Vergilian models; the nature of Livy's historical enterprise; the uses of moral history in comparison with that of Herodotus and Thucydides.

Pedagogical issues: Comparing historiographical method, narrative technique, and persuasive rhetorical usage.

UNIT 7: CHRISTIANITY AND LATE ANTIQUITY

After Livy we take another huge leap. There is a lot missing: we do not cover much of the later centuries of the Roman empire (as intriguing as they are) save as they affect the development of Christian literature. This is not because there is nothing there to study, but because there is only so much one *can* cover in a thirty-five week course.

With the coming of Christianity, most of our students seem more comfortable. Many of them also probably make assumptions about it that they cannot afford to make, because, being Christians themselves, they may think that they are more familiar with the makeup of the early church than they really are. Accordingly, I try first to provide some reference points, and then to move out from there.

Please bear in mind in all that follows that I am *not* trying to bring a particular sectarian belief to bear here. We have Catholics and Protestants in our classes, and some adherents of other faiths, and they all bring different suppositions to the table. I'm perfectly happy with that, and encourage genuine dialogue between them, as long as it all remains courteous and respectful. So far we have managed to have that happen; I hope it will remain that way.

WEEK 23: EARLY CHRISTIAN WRITINGS

The first year or two I taught this course I had at least one Protestant parent raise an objection to the Catholic indoctrination I was obviously providing by presenting the text of the Catholic Mass. Please let me clarify: I'm a Protestant myself, but there is no way to look honestly at the first fifteen hundred years of the Christian experience in Europe *without* taking into account what the Catholic Church was doing, and why. The text of the Mass was a set of words heard and used every week (or more often) by most of the Christians throughout Europe. There is no other single formulation of words, ideas, and even rhythms of speech, that left so large an imprint on the minds of those who used words and ideas, and who, along the way, generated much of the literature we are studying from this point on.

Yes: inasmuch as I'm a Protestant from a liturgical-tradition church, I confess I find little or nothing to object to in the words of the Mass (and in fact, divorced from their contexts, neither do most Christians from confessional/reformed traditions), but I'm offering them in order to teach something important about cultural history of these ages, not in order to indoctrinate anyone furtively in points of faith. I enthusiastically leave that job up to you, the parents, to perform openly and unapologetically according to the lights of your own beliefs.

The Latin Mass (which is given on the website) is given in both Latin and in translation; parts of it go back to pre-Christian Judaic prayers and formulae. It's worth remembering that Christians were using at least some of these prayers from the very first days after Our Lord's resurrection and ascension, long before the texts we regard as scripture existed at all.

Alongside this, we also go through the Gospel of Mark. There are a few reasons for this — first of all, Mark's Gospel is often thought to have been the first one written, and so has a primacy of place on those grounds. It is also the shortest, and hence easiest to read right through. I have also always found reading it through in one sitting to be a remarkably bracing experience. To that extent (and without sectarian bias at all) I commend it to all Christians. If that doesn't provide your faith with a shot in the arm, I don't know what will.

Finally, I have also added to this week's reading the second chapter of Auerbach's *Mimesis*. It is not a chapter we discuss very extensively, but it covers certain very useful points, and helps develop the critical vocabulary he will use in later chapters, so it's important not to skip it. Again, if it makes no sense on first reading, don't worry about it, but don't write it off as nonsense, either. It really does have a clear value.

> *Topical issues*: Christ as hero and hero transformed; comparison of the heroes and martyrs of the Christian faith with the heroes of the Old Testament, and with the Homeric, Livian, and Vergilian models.

> *Pedagogical issues*: Achieving enough distance to look at this material objectively; seeing how the scripture of the Christian Church came to be put together.

WEEK 24: AUGUSTINE

Augustine of Hippo (354-430) was a loose-living young man with more learning than good sense; he taught rhetoric, believed in nothing much, and fathered at least one child out of wedlock; then he was converted, and by a remarkable series of transformations became one of the most persuasive apologists and theologians in the history of Christianity.

Augustine accomplished a number of things as a priest and bishop in his own day, but his writing is the most enduring part of his legacy.

Up to this point in history, there has probably been no author — with the possible fitful exception of Cicero — who presented *himself* as clearly as did Augustine. His writings of all sorts are straightforward, well-reasoned, and intensely honest. His *Confessions* in particular are the model (seldom if ever surpassed) of spiritual autobiography. He is brutally honest about his own shortcomings, and neither wallows in mere sentimentality nor attempts to justify himself. In short, his work is unique and powerful. Usually this assignment falls sometime in the season of Lent, and, for those who observe Lent with particular spiritual disciplines, there could be few better than a reading of the *Confessions* entire.

We are also looking this week at the third chapter of Mimesis, and it introduces a couple of fairly simple ideas with seventy-five-cent names: *parataxis* and *hypotaxis*. Clarifying the distinction between the two usually entails a short excursion into the land of grammatical theory, but since this is (in the broader sense) an English course, that seems justifiable. *Parataxis* refers to the construction of prose made up primarily of independent or coordinate clauses, with a minimum of subordinate clauses. *Hypotaxis* refers to the construction of prose that contains a much higher concentration of subordinate clauses. Where this leads us in terms of the literary analysis of the text is intriguing, I think, and will have ramifications for several weeks to come. But if your student doesn't pick it all up on the first reading, don't become fretful. We'll plan to go over it in class.

> *Topical issues*: The personal voice of the writer; the heroism of the faith. Parataxis and hypotaxis as indicators of an underlying conception of reality

Pedagogical issues: Careful reading of prose in order to discern its structure and makeup, with a view toward seeing the author's view of reality as expressed in concrete particulars of grammatical usage.

WEEK 25: BENEDICT OF NURSIA, BOËTHIUS

This pairing of authors and works is largely a matter of convenience and temporal coincidence. Boëthius and Benedict have very little in common in terms of literary training, aspirations, methodology, or much else — though it is generally believed that both were Christians. (Of Benedict there is no real room for doubt; there have been those who question the authenticity of Boëthius' theological writings.)

The *Regula Benedicti* is one of the foundational documents of the intellectual and cultural life of the Latin Middle Ages. Part of this has to do with its position: it was from this rule and this definition of the monastic life that most monasteries in Europe sprang. There were other varieties of monastic and eremetic life in the Greek-speaking eastern Mediterranean, but the monastic movement was fairly unformed in Europe when Benedict founded his order at Montecassino (Italy), and the Benedictine form of monasticism eclipsed the rest for many generations, and remains to this day the primary historical impulse to the common contemplative life. Partly Benedictine monasticism succeeded due to its extraordinary practicality: far from being a deeply spiritual document in any abstract sense, the *Rule* addresses mostly the day-to-day aspects of running a community of people; and even today people with no particular interest in the monastic life, or even in Christianity, have found it a useful and enlightening textbook in personnel management — more detailed than many, and more humane than most. Benedict writes all this in a workmanlike Latin prose that aspires only to a utilitarian clarity; and yet, because it was read aloud in daily portions, three times a year, every year, its phrases became part and parcel of the monks' grasp of their language — it entered every part of their discourse, surpassed only by the phrasings of the Psalms. And so, in an unanticipated way, Benedict became a model of Latin style to the Middle Ages.

Boëthius, on the other hand, was a member of a high-ranking senatorial family, and he had had the benefits of the best literary, rhetorical, and philosophical education the time could afford. He writes an elegant Latin; he is conversant in classical forms of poetry, and he uses them with ease and finesse. The problem he is facing, to be sure, is no less practical than the one facing Benedict, and a good deal more pressing: he has been imprisoned on charges of treason by the Ostrogothic king Theodoric Amal (the Ostrogoths have taken over from the Visigoths, ruled by Odoacer or Odovacar, who deposed the last Roman emperor Romulus Augustulus in 476). Whether there is anything to these charges is hard, at this distance, to determine. Possibly it involved no more than communicating with members of the imperial court in Byzantium. In prison, however, he had time to do little other than to think and write — and this book is the result. It has been one of the most celebrated pieces of prison literature — a vast and highly motivated genre taking in things from some of the letters of Paul to Hitler's *Mein Kampf*, Malory's *Morte D'Arthur* to Martin Luther King's "Letter from a Birmingham Jail". Though it is not widely read nowadays, it was certainly one of the most important books for the mediaeval reader.

Boëthius survived long enough to complete the book, which is a *Menippean satire* — alternating passages of poetry and prose — constituting a philosophical defense of the notion that we are not, in any really important sense, subject to fortune. Having reached this conclusion, he was then executed by the gruesome expedient of having cords twisted around his head until it was crushed. But his work has survived and left an enormous mark: while it has been dismissed by some as philosophically unoriginal, it clearly has made some of the traditional philosophical ideas accessible to people in adverse situations. Chaucer translated it into English, as did Elizabeth Tudor — herself under house arrest — before she became Elizabeth I of England.

We do not have time to do justice to either of these works, really, but both of them are sufficiently important to deserve some treatment. We discuss the main topics of each, and try to look at the forms each take, and how that form affects the work's use. We generally also have to do a bit of discussion of the nature of monasticism (and what is *not* monasticism), since a number of students — even among the Catholics — are fairly unclear on its boundaries.

> *Topical issues*: Philosophy and theology — how are they connected? Persuasive rhetoric directed at oneself: *cf.* Lucretius. A practical manual: the birth of the how-to book?
>
> *Pedagogical issues*: Distinguishing different modes of composition and different compositional purposes and forms.

WEEK 26: GREGORY OF TOURS; *HILDEBRANDSLIED*

Not much later than Boëthius and Benedict, but somewhat farther north, we find bishop Gregory laboring away as bishop of Tours, a city in Gaul now held by the Franks. Gregory writes his *Historia Francorum* in a Latin as appallingly bad as can be found. His historiographical purpose, when compared with that of Herodotus, Thucydides, or Livy, seems relatively unambitious: he mostly just seems to want to get the facts down so that someone will remember. Most of the time he succeeds, and he has succeeded in his modest goal: his work is one of our only sources for large stretches of early Frankish history.

Through it, however, emerges something rather remarkable. Despite his awkward Latin, filled with grammatical barbarisms and freakish spellings, he manages to achieve considerable personal gravity and seriousness, and the story he tells is strangely compelling. True, he doesn't know how to tell it very well; he sometimes leads the reader into obscure verbal quagmires where all pronouns seem to be pointing at different things, but it's impossible to tell which one is pointing at which thing, or sentences with dangling modifiers that lead nowhere. But in a deeper sense, he does seem to share the goals of his more illustrious predecessors: he's writing moral history, emphasizing and trying to make sense out of the moral constants of the universe and of his faith. In his way he's wrestling with the same questions that have troubled all the historians we've read, as well as people like Aeschylus, Euripides, Augustine, Boëthius, and the author of Job: what is the connection, if any, between moral action and real-world consequences?

Gregory also occasions what is my own personal favorite among Auerbach's chapters: the fourth, "Sicharius and Chramnesindus", takes a charitable and occasionally profound look at how Gregory brought his surroundings to life and committed them to writing.

Added to this selection almost as an afterthought, but in fact bridging to the next section, is a translation of the oldest surviving Old High German poem, the *Hildebrandslied*. I have two purposes here: one is to try to show how the early Germanic tribes dealt with things: another is to show through another instance just how tightly-knit the fabric of early Germanic legend was. In effect, it is the Trojan War story of a completely different cultural group. The Theotrihhe mentioned here is none other than the Theodoric who had Boëthius executed, and who will show up again in the Middle High German *Nibelungenlied* as Dietrich von Bern. Hildebrand himself shows up in the later poem, too. As in the Trojan War stories, there is clearly a layer of historical truth, upon which all manner of fiction has been hatched.

As a work of art on its own, the *Hildebrandslied*, only a few dozen lines, is an interesting challenge. It's only a fragment: though it almost certainly begins where what we have begins, its ending is missing. From what we know of the poem and its culture, how should we assume it will turn out?

> *Topical issues*: The hero of the faith in the new Christian era: heroism in the primitive Germanic mold; how these are compared to one another and to the other models of the hero we've seen to date. Morality as manifested in the world. *Hildebrandslied*: early Germanic alliterative poetics.

> *Pedagogical issues*: Discerning a common purpose; dealing with fragmentary texts.

UNIT 8: THE HEROIC MIDDLE AGES

This unit — like the next one — is named fairly arbitrarily to correspond roughly with the material I've gathered to put into it. It represents literature from both the Christian and pagan Germanic traditions, but most of the works are landmarks that ought not to be overlooked. It represents a variety of forms — epic of sorts and saga, and the so-called *chanson de geste*, a quasi-epic French form based moderately closely on history. It draws on a variety of the basic stories — no more from the Trojan War tales, but from both the Arthurian matter and from the old Germanic myth of Sigurd/Siegfried and all his surrounding kindred and their strife — a tale that grows out of the early encounters of the Franks and Goths with the Huns, during the fifth century and after. It also contains the greatest piece of the (much larger) cycle of Carolingian stories (those concerning Charlemagne), the *Song of Roland*, a *chanson de geste* from about the year 1000.

WEEK 27: THE *SONG OF ROLAND*

This is one of the most famous works of the Middle Ages, and one of the first works written in a language that can legitimately be called French. It tells the tragic tale of a pair of Charlemagne's paladins who are effectively tricked into commanding a rear-guard on a trip through the Pyrenees, while Charlemagne is doing battle with the Muslim kingdoms of Spain; they are slaughtered, in part through their unfortunate position, and in part through Roland's own unwillingness to call for help when he needs it.

As a work of literature it is at once electrifying and disorienting. It tells a riveting narrative that is nonetheless beset with inexplicable repetitions and odd bits of indirection that seem to lead nowhere. It is based on some shadowy historical events, though nobody is quite sure what happened, really — the best theory to date seems to be that it was a tribe of Basques that wiped out the Emperor's rear-guard, rather than Moorish forces; and certainly when the event is supposed to have taken place, Charles himself was probably in his mid-thirties — not, as the poem reports, in excess of 200.

The poem is a case study in how epic language can coalesce around historical events and permute them to a more poetical shape. We discuss the interconnection of the historical and the poetic here.

We also have once again the occasion to look at yet another kind of hero. Roland is a Christian military hero — both a warrior and a defender of the faith. Just how the author of the poem apprehended the Christian faith is occasionally quite perplexing: at least it is a bit unclear how he saw the differences between Christianity and Islam, since he fills his depiction of Islamic society with priests and bishops and has those clergy celebrating a Muslim Mass. Be that as it may, the picture that emerges of Roland is intriguing, and represents a different kind of hero still, not unlike the early Roman community-centered hero, but tinged with an odd vanity that puts the Christianity on a shaky footing. Morality is a given: Christians are (generally) good, and Muslims are (invariably) bad, but the terms of good and evil are seldom in fact discussed or evaluated.

Finally, we have another chapter of Auerbach to read: we seldom get a chance to discuss it here very thoroughly, but it should provide some contextualizing perspective.

Topical issues: The Christian secular hero as warrior and mar-
tyr; characterization in a morally polarized story. Interlocked
history and myth, and how each shapes the other. The tragic
and epic components of this story *vs.* those of Greek tragedy
and epic.

Pedagogical issues: Examining *how* a story is told for clues
about its underlying vision of reality. What does discontinu-
ity tell us?

WEEK 28: THE *VOLSUNGA SAGA*

This is a purely pagan product of the early Germanic story — the
first time we will see it told — in Iceland, which was very late to be
converted to Christianity. It tells a raw and unvarnished story in sinewy and businesslike prose (with here and there a snippet of poetry)
about several generations of a family ultimately derived from the chief
god Odin — their rise, their dealings with varieties of treason domestic
and foreign, and their ultimate extinction. It originally derives from
historic fact, too: Sigurd is not known from history as such, but many
of the peripheral characters are. Atli, for example, is the famous Hun
Attila.

It is the first and only example of *saga* literature we have time to
cover; in fact there are many out there, most of them worth reading. I
selected this not because it is the greatest or the most famous (it's not
— probably that distinction goes to *Njal's Saga*, an amazing piece of
work) but precisely because it *is* linked to the story that informs the
Nibelungenlied, much of the *Elder Edda*, and touches such narratives as

the *Hildebrandslied, Beowulf,* and is even preserved into the nineteenth century, in a permuted form, in Wagner's *Der Ring des Nibelungen.*

The story is an undiluted — even brutal — pagan product of a less refined sensibility than one finds in Homer. It describes (not in any kind of provocative detail, of course) at least one instance of incest, a variety of colorful forms of murder within families, and suicide as well. None of this is presented as being commendable, to be sure, nor do we suggest anything of the sort in class. One of my chief reasons for showing this at all is to allow the student to compare this version with the later *Nibelungenlied,* which is basically the same story, but retold from a Christian perspective, and marked by radically different social and moral expectations. Seeing how stories are reworked and warped over time is one of the main themes of this course.

> *Topical issues*: The pagan Germanic hero and the values of the heroic culture as compared with those of Homer *et al.* The nature of the saga medium.

> *Pedagogical issues*: Seeing how stories are permuted through various forms.

WEEK 29: THE *NIBELUNGENLIED*

The anonymous *Nibelungenlied* is the Middle High German rendition of the same story as that of the *Volsunga Saga*; it has come under the influence of contemporary French sensibilities, in particular a new-found fascination with the romance form — which we have a first look at next week. (There is no way to work all the bits of the schedule out so that the pieces all come in the best order: I'd like to have the Chré-tien de Troyes before this reading, but also want to link this with the last week's *Volsunga Saga*, while allowing Chrétien to lead us into Dante — somewhere one has to compromise.)

Like the *Song of Roland*, the *Nibelungenlied* is one of the small hand-ful of almost universally acknowledged masterpieces of mediaeval literature. It is not without its defects, though, and perhaps the greatest source of internal friction derives precisely from the fact that it is trying to express ancient epic or saga material in the form of a romance, which is really incapable of sustaining it. Up to the approximate half-way point, the experiment nearly works, but then it collapses under the burden of the darkening narrative: it doesn't fail completely, but the illusion of romance is shattered and replaced by a conviction of tragic and inescapable doom. In the end, it may be one of the great failures of mediaeval literature — but certainly a grand one — and it manages to climb in its awkward way to lyric heights and flashes of brilliant and memorable characterization.

The *Nibelungenlied* is rather long, so I have not required it all. In-stead, I have made a patchwork translation of some of the most critical parts, derived from an old public-domain translation that I have my-self tried to repair and turn into something like modern English. It is very stilted indeed. I definitely recommend that students who are par-ticularly interested in this get the Hatto translation (Penguin Classics) and read it through — but certainly we won't be examining anyone on the remaining contents.

Topical issues: The romance hero *vs.* the epic hero; how the medium can (or cannot) affect the content of the message.

Pedagogical issues: Determining an author's biases and aspirations, and trying to see how they may affect his final product.

UNIT 9: ROMANCE AND MYSTICISM

This last unit contains some of the easiest, and also some of the most difficult, material we cover all year. The *Yvain* of Chrétien de Troyes is a bit of a romp — not particularly challenging, but quite entertaining, and perhaps typifying, as well as anything can, the character of the romance form. From there we move on to some difficult theoretical material in the form of critical interpretive philosophy by both St. Thomas Aquinas and Dante Alighieri, in what is probably the most interpretively challenging week of the year — after which we arrive at the greatest mediaeval romance of them all, which is yet not quite a romance either: Dante's *Divine Comedy*.

WEEK 30: CHRÉTIEN DE TROYES

Chrétien de Troyes is the author that the most students have pointed to, in later years, as their favorite discovery from this course. He is certainly not the greatest, but he is able to tell a rip-roaring good yarn, and he delivers it with such grace and style that one is swept along for page after page by the sheer delight of his writing. The *Yvain* is only one of five surviving Arthurian romances by Chrétien: all of them are now much easier to find than they once were, and are available in several good editions. Anyone who wants to make any further study of mediaeval romance as such (*e.g.*, the other romances of the French tradition, such as Beroul's *Tristan*, or the *Lais* of Marie de France, or the German Arthurian materials such as Wolfram von Eschenbach's *Parzival*, Gottfried von Strassburg's *Tristan*, or the various

works of Hartmann von Aue) would be well-advised to read the Chrétien collection right through. There's not time for that here, though, so
we confine ourselves to the most salient parts of this one work.

Ideally, everyone would read the whole of the *Yvain*; there is no
practical way to excerpt bits to form a condensed "good parts" version
— one really has to begin at the beginning and go on from there. I do
realize that not everyone is *able* to read the whole in a single week, and
so I tend to emphasize mostly the early parts of the story in our work.
We talk about probability in narrative, and the alternate landscape that
frames the whole of this poem (and others like it) — using Auerbach's
chapter as a point of reference.

Ultimately this romance — like all romances — is a kind of comedy
of manners, or in its most serious moments, a moral essay on how one
ought to behave. It is worth approaching the poem with this in mind: it
allows comparison with many of the other works we've discussed so
far (the *Nibelungenlied*, which takes after Chrétien in many superficial
ways, cannot possibly be interpreted in this way; neither can most ancient epic, including the *Odyssey*, despite Homer's preoccupation there
with being a good guest or a good host). In some ways, the work has
more in common with many older historical works, and it sets up
some context to appreciate the *Divine Comedy* as a moral work.

Topical issues: The romance hero as distinct from the epic
hero; Christian morality *vs.* courtly ethics: where are the
boundaries? Man and nature in the romance.

Pedagogical issues: Again, discerning the author's main interest in a narrative, and finding how that is expressed.

WEEK 31: THOMAS AQUINAS AND DANTE ALIGHIERI

This week is probably the most difficult theoretical crossroads of the course: it zeroes in on the philosophical question, "How does a narrative mean anything?" This is important to understanding what Dante is up to, to be sure, and it's a question that any of us ought to consider in dealing with literature of any sort. It also helps, I think, to put into context what we have been saying all along about *ecphrasis* and other forms of included or embedded narrative, and how its capacity to generate meanings can be projected onto the fabric of the enclosing narrative.

To get to the root of the question, we go back to a fundamental issue for Christians: how scripture carries meaning in particular. In the process, we turn to Thomas Aquinas' masterwork, the *Summa Theologica*, looking carefully at Question I.1.10, which discusses whether and how a passage of scripture can support more than one sense.

I'm not expecting most students to grasp the central issue of this question on a first or even a second reading: we will go over it in class in some detail, to determine what exactly Aquinas is driving at, and also to measure it against some of the background ideas of the early Middle Ages (deriving from the Augustinian/Alexandrian exegetical models). What emerges should, I think, put into context a number of issues that have been at the boundaries of the course throughout the year, and also provide some real challenge for the student's own understanding of scripture.

As I have had occasion to point out before, my own interest in bringing this material up here is *not* to indoctrinate anyone. Aquinas is indeed widely regarded as the chief theological thinker in the history of the Catholic church, and his ideas deserve a great deal of respect and scrutiny to this day by Catholics and Protestants alike; but I'm certainly not trying to convert anyone to any particular position. But Thomas here asks a singularly important question, and I think that (whatever conclusion one reaches) an honest Christian needs to confront that question for himself. It is important for us to know, as believers, *how* do the scriptures express God's meaning?

The remaining work is uniquely placed as an interpretive key to the *Divine Comedy*, since it gives Dante's own rationale for writing it the way he has, and it forms at least a partial key to understanding it. We have nothing like this for any other work of literature we've read all year, and the opportunity is not to be missed. It also picks up and plays with many of the ideas that have come up in the selection from Aquinas, so it helps round out the picture.

None of this is easy reading, but it's relatively short, and I try to make sure that all the students grasp the relevant distinctions in the class discussion.

> *Topical issues*: Text *vs.* referent: what bears the meaning?

> *Pedagogical issues*: A primarily philosophical set of issues relating to signification.

WEEK 32: DANTE, *DIVINE COMEDY* 1: INFERNO

Finally we come to the great Italian poet, polymath, and politician who has so generously (if unintentionally) lent his name to our course.

Dante Alighieri was a Florentine, and eventually an exile from Florence, during a period of enormous upheaval in the political and religious life of northern Italy. The papacy was going into exile in Avignon, from which it didn't return until late in the 1300s; the major cities of Tuscany (especially Florence) were divided into factions, some favoring strengthening the connection with the Holy Roman Empire (*i.e.*, modern Austria, which still had some claim over parts of northern Italy), and some opposing it.

Into this turbulent and confusing situation, Dante came as a writer, a mystic, and a political agitator. He was the first of his time to dare to write a serious work in Italian, thus establishing the Tuscan dialect of the language as standard Italian down to this day. He was by turns brilliant and petty; willfully blind and prodigiously visionary, managing to be magnanimous and spiteful all within the space of a few lines. One senses that he gloated a little bit when placing his enemies (some of them still alive) in one or another pit of Hell, and felt vindicated by what he managed to contrive.

At the same time, his work is both the culmination of the mediaeval romantic vision, since it represents the ultimate quest (leading as it does through all the eternal realms and confronting all human moral conditions), and its end, since it renders almost impossible any return to the mental world of a Chrétien.

Like Chrétien's romances, the *Divine Comedy* is a moral work, primarily, played out on an internal landscape. It's framed as an allegory, to be sure, but its chief purpose is to disclose something about man's moral relationship with the world and with God. In doing so it equates — not unnaturally, but rather elliptically — a man's *character* with his *destiny*. This is a point Auerbach made earlier in his career in the book, *Dante als Dichter der irdischen Welt* — translated as *Dante, Poet of the Secular World*. This peculiar assessment of Dante is one that bears some investigation. It probably goes without saying that anyone who devotes so much space to a vision of the Christian afterlife is almost definitionally not a secularist — but what Auerbach is driving at is valid in a certain light.

The chapter from Auerbach is among the most intriguing and useful in the collection: again, if the student can grasp it, great; if not, we can talk. It is worth re-reading a few times, though, to see what one can find there.

> *Topical issues*: The spiritual quest and the romance hero as compared with the gospels' and the Old Testament's vision of the spiritual hero. Characterization through time and in an eternal context.

> *Pedagogical issues*: Understanding the limits of a type of discourse, and the problematic poetics of writing about the eternal.

WEEK 33: DANTE, *DIVINE COMEDY* 2: PURGATORIO

I find myself in an odd position here as a Protestant: though the doctrine of Purgatory is not an integral part of my faith at all, I find (as do many others) that this middle book of the *Divine Comedy* is in many ways my favorite. I think this is because the experiences of the souls in Purgatory as depicted here are in fact most like that of the souls in this world — they are *en route* somewhere, subject to change, responsive to spiritual forces, and capable of growth and renewal. Where they are when we see them is *not* their final destination; the character-as-destiny fabric is here probably at its thinnest. That appeals to me, and certainly reflects my experience of this world.

> *Topical issues*: The hero's progress and development; moral issues in temporal *vs.* eternal frameworks.

> *Pedagogical issues*: How the content of the different parts of a work help shape its tone and its approach to its work.

WEEK 34: DANTE, *DIVINE COMEDY: PARADISO*

Many students find this the least interesting part of the *Divine Comedy*, and, inasmuch as it is chiefly a kind of prolonged ecstatic vision of paradise, this is probably not surprising. If one is caught up in the vision, it can be quite overwhelming; if one is not, it seems merely to offer wave upon wave of superlatives. It does, however, complete the totality of Dante's vision, and gives us yet another context to view the character-as-destiny equation.

We talk about all these themes, and also use the time to try to piece together a synthetic vision of what Dante has done throughout the whole of the *Divine Comedy*.

> *Topical issues*: Mystical and ecstatic utterance in poetry; visions of the whole of the mediaeval world-view.

> *Pedagogical issues*: Putting together the pieces of a large asymmetrical work like the *Divine Comedy*.

[WEEK 35: REVIEW]

I attempt in the review session to open discussion to student questions of all sorts. We also discuss the final exam and its peculiar format, with a few example question to get students onto the right track.

AFTERWORD

This overview by no means exhausts all the material we go through in the course, but it should suffice to keep you in touch with what your children are reading and learning, and perhaps give you something to discuss with them — both for your own amusement and to follow how they are doing in their studies. Feel free to follow up these questions, and to go into more detail; if you have questions that leave you puzzled yourself, feel free to write me. I can't promise I'll know the answer, but I probably have some resources you don't, and may be able to help tracking the answers down. In any case, we can open the discourse on a wider footing, which is all to the good.

The purpose of the course, as will be seen in retrospect, is not to provide anything like an exhaustive view of this enormous stretch of literary history: that would be impossible in ten such courses. A full command even of the small selection of works we've read here is not possible in so little time, either. I understand that, and so should you. But the course will have succeeded if it opens up the field, so that the students feel free and empowered (a much overused term, but still valid) to go back to these works and beyond them in their own reading, and if they have learned how to approach them with critical minds and discerning analysis. These are far from dead pieces of literature: that they are still available and being read today is, if anything, proof of an extraordinary vitality. They ask questions that real people are wrestling with at all times, and they are a common living heritage and foundation of world culture: we may never master them entirely, but the effort to try can be vastly rewarding.

ANNOTATED BIBLIOGRAPHY

This bibliography falls into two distinct sections: the first is a discussion of the texts we use in the class; the second is a more extensive (but less well-annotated) listing of other books for follow-up reading in case any of these things catches your attention.

COURSE TEXTS

What follows is mostly a list of the texts assigned for the course, both optional and required — something about their content, as well as my reasons for choosing a particular translation (where that option is relevant). In most cases, the selections were the result of examining a good number of other translations: I have tried in practical terms to balance the costs of the course against the utility of each book.

Homer, *The Iliad*, tr. Robert Fagles (New York, Penguin Books, 1990). ISBN 0-14-044592-7.

— , *The Odyssey*, tr. E.V. Rieu and D. C. H. Rieu (New York, Penguin Books, 1991). ISBN 0-14-044556-0.

There is simply no translation of Homer that captures the peculiar resonance and clarity of Homeric diction in its original Greek form. The ones I have chose here are not particularly better than the others in an absolute sense; their virtues are that they both aim at clarity and accessibility, and are less intimidating than many another translation might be. Especially in the first major work we encounter in the course, those virtues seemed important.

Fagles' translations of both the *Iliad* and the *Odyssey* have been received with great acclaim by the reading public at large, and some amount of grumbling in the classics community. In fact, I think they are neither as good nor as bad as some on either extreme would like to claim. They are intended to make the poems lively and accessible, with occasional recourse to modern diction that approaches slanginess around the edges — a decision that is not at all reflective of Homer's highly artificial art language. Nevertheless, it does *succeed* in those goals: it really does make the text lively, and most first-time readers find that it helps, especially through some of the longer and more arid passages, and through the relentless *aristeia*-mongering that Homer indulges in the poem's midsection.

I chose the Rieu translation of the *Odyssey* for contrasting reasons. Like Fagles' *Iliad*, it is reasonably accessible, but it's a prose translation, devoid of the slightest pretense of poetic language. I selected it in part to emphasize a point that students often have a hard time grasping: that though these are both poems to start with, the form they assume in translation is largely an artifact of the translator's work, and should not be trusted to express anything about the form of the Greek. In further defense of the Rieu translation, however, I can say that it's reasonably accurate to the poet's sense: I accordingly recommend it to my Greek students who are wrestling with the *Odyssey* in Greek. Finally, I have found that the prose format makes for somewhat easier reading — an advantage in the part of the course where the students first encounter Auerbach's *Mimesis*, which can be more than a little intimidating.

The range of options on Homer translations is enormous, however, and if you are of an adventurous disposition, they are worth checking out. One can find still in print Thomas Chapman's original English translation (about which John Keats waxed so lyrical in his sonnet "On First Looking into Chapman's Homer") or Alexander

Pope's mannered translation into English heroic couplets. Samuel Butler's workmanlike and uninspiring rendition into prose is available almost everywhere, from Barnes and Noble's reprint line to Project Gutenberg on the Worldwide Web. There continue to be new translations every few years; perhaps the closest to the original in metrical form is that of Richmond Lattimore — which is difficult going in spots, but attempts to preserve something of the rhythms of Greek hexameter line. W. H. D. Rouse's translations in the Mentor line are to be approached skeptically, as they are perilously close to being paraphrases, with a lot cut out. Remarkably good and grossly under-appreciated are the blank verse versions of the nineteenth-century American poet William Cullen Bryant (whose "Thanatopsis" is a staple of high school American literature courses everywhere — including our own); the only drawback for students at this level is that he insists on using the Roman names of characters and gods, which can prove temporarily disorienting. One can get past that, but to the best of my knowledge, these versions are currently out of print. Perhaps some enterprising person will put them out once again, or at least scan them in as part of Project Gutenberg.

E. R. Lind, ed., *Ten Greek Plays in Contemporary Translation*. (Boston, Houghton-Mifflin, 1957). ISBN 0-395-05117-7.

This under-appreciated little volume contains some remarkably decent translations of several Greek plays. From it we read several items: Aeschylus' *Agamemnon*, Sophocles' *Oedipus Rex* and *Antigone*, and Euripides' *Bacchae*. We have to resort to web translations for Aeschylus' *Eumenides* (and *Choephoroi/Libation Bearers*, for those who choose to read it), and Euripides' *Helen*. They tend not to be as good as the ones found here.

There are alternative sources for all of these, of course. The best general repository of Greek tragedy in English today is the collection edited by Richmond Lattimore and David Grene, which contain faithful and gritty translations of all the surviving works of Aeschylus, Sophocles, and Euripides. They are available in a variety of formats — in four hardback volumes totaling about $200, or in a stack of paperbacks containing a few plays each, and probably (taken together) costing even more.

In addition, the *Oresteia* of Aeschylus and the Theban plays (*Oedipus Rex [Tyrannus], Oedipus at Colonus,* and *Antigone*)of Sophocles have been translated by Robert Fagles (Penguin), whose *Iliad* we use (see above), and also by Paul Roche (Mentor). I have never been particularly fond of the Roche translations, and the Fagles versions seem almost overly colloquial to me, but these things are a matter of taste.

Virgil, *The Aeneid,* tr. David West (New York, Penguin, 1991). ISBN 0-14-044457-2.

The most common translations of the *Aeneid* in academia now are probably the Fitzgerald and Mandelbaum translations, which both have considerable virtues to commend them, but the West translation is remarkably faithful to the text of the original, and as a prose translation it can maintain that fidelity without attempting to interpose another poetic sensibility of its own. It's not perfect for all purposes, but I have generally found it better to give this fairly plain version to students, while taking those students who were willing and able through the genuine article later on in AP Latin IV. Nobody has ever captured the grandeur and subtlety of the Vergilian hexameter in English.

Anon., *The Song of Roland*, tr. Glyn Burgess (London, Penguin Books, 1990). ISBN 0-14-044532-3.

There are a number of translations of the *Song of Roland* on the market now, and most of them have various virtues. I have tended to shy away from the more singsong versions, and accordingly I'm not particularly fond of Dorothy L. Sayers', which is a favorite of many homeschoolers. The translations by Patricia Terry or Frederic Bliss Luquiens are worth checking out, but very hard to find nowadays. The new Burgess version seemed a good compromise.

Anon., *Saga of the Volsungs*, tr. Jesse Byock (New York, Penguin Books, 2000). ISBN 0-14-044738-5.

For many years the only English version of this was the translation of the nineteenth-century artist and aesthete William Morris (known for diverse crafts, including type design, wallpaper manufacture, poetry, painting, and even an early form of the recliner.) While one cannot help marveling at Morris's industry and ingenuity, his translation is arch and full of sixteenth-century language that, while it may have spoken to the late nineteenth century of the heroic Germanic past, really points nowhere now. It was with great relief that I discovered that the very sound translation by Prof. Byock, at first published in a higher-priced edition through the University of California, had been released by Penguin Classics. He preserves the bald clarity of the original gritty, gruesome tale.

Dante Alighieri, *The Portable Dante*, tr. Mark Musa. New York, Penguin Books, 1995. ISBN 0-14-023114-5.

To grasp Dante in his original purity, one wants to learn Italian. Dante's *Divine Comedy* has been translated over and over, but never successfully. Like Homer, Dante has a water-clear diction that eludes everyone, every time — even as they see it slipping away. Longfellow gave the project a good try, but it doesn't really work, I think; I positively dislike Dorothy Sayers' version (though her notes are in many ways the best set published for the general reader), largely because of her insistence on preserving the *terza rima* of the Italian — a virtually impossible feat to pull off in English. Sayers' version is still in print, and still worth acquiring for the notes. The real Dante fan will probably want to go for the three (now published as six) volumes in the Princeton-Bollingen series by Singleton, preserving both the Italian text and a flatly literal English prose translation, together with very extensive notes on almost every aspect of the poem. But that's a fairly major investment, running to well over a hundred dollars in paperback.

So I have settled on Mark Musa's translation, which is published in three volumes as part of the Penguin Classics series, or here, in one. I'm not entirely happy with this translation, either, but it does manage to catch a lot of the idiomatic clarity of the Italian, and puts it into a blank verse with enough rhythm to feel like poetry.

Erich Auerbach, *Mimesis*, tr. Willard Trask. (Princeton, 1953). ISBN 0-691-01269-5.

Erich Auerbach was a German Jew who was fortunate enough to escape the rising tide of Nazism; he wrote this astounding book in Istanbul, where he spent World War II, with access to only the most minimal research facilities. He later claimed that, had he had a better library, *Mimesis* almost certainly would never have seen the light of day. As it was, it did, and it remains one of the genuinely unique works of literary criticism and evaluation in the twentieth century.

The Bible, in any good modern translation.

I especially recommend the New International Version for its literal accuracy; the Revised Standard is also acceptable. The King James is really not quite faithful enough; the New Revised Standard seems to me to be full of agenda-based (politically correct) errors. You almost certainly have your own household standard, though, and in general I'd prefer not to interfere with anyone's selection.

Anon., *The Nibelungenlied*, tr. A. T. Hatto (London, Penguin Books, 1965, 1969). ISBN 0-14-044137-9.

This is much more approachable than the stilted translation from which I have excerpted passages. We are not, however, reading the entire work, and you may not find it worth your while to buy this. I have made it optional.

PRINT SOURCES FOR READINGS NOT IN THE ASSIGNED
BOOKS

I've provided access through the web to everything in the course
outside the required texts, but for those who really prefer reading from
the page, here are some options on other materials. In general, I've fa-
vored the most accessible versions. (I'm not getting a kickback from
Penguin Books, but the Penguin Classics series is available in almost
every large bookstore across the country, and it covers a remarkable
breadth of material, sometimes in multiple versions.) Obviously if you
buy all these volumes, you will be adding a good deal to the cost of the
course, but that's your business; I think I can claim that they are all
worth having and reading (except as otherwise noted).

Richmond Lattimore, David Grene, et al., *The Complete Greek Tragedies.*
Various editions.

The plays of Aeschylus, Sophocles, and Euripides are available
in many editions, and you're free to explore for those that suit you.
Probably the best of the lot are still these editions (four volumes in
hardback; published in several different paperback configurations)
from the University of Chicago. There are too many different forms
to warrant listing all the separate ISBNs. These are highly likely to
be available in some form in your local public or university library.
The full hardbound set is rather pricy, though quite good.

Herodotus, *The Histories*, tr. Aubrey de Sélincourt, rev. John M. Marincola. (London, Penguin Books, 1996). ISBN 0-14-044638-9.

— , *The Landmark Herodotus*, tr. Richard Crawley. (New York, Pantheon, 2007). pb. ISBN 1-40-003114-1; hb. ISBN 0-37-542109-2.

An old standby translation that has been part of the Penguin Classics series for several generations, newly revised and corrected. Herodotus is widely readable and generally entertaining; one can dip into his fabric of strange and wonderful stories almost anywhere and find something interesting to read.

The Landmark Herodotus is built on the model of the earlier *Landmark Thucydides*, and is liberally supplied with maps that should significantly ease the difficulties of locating what is going on where in Herodotus.

Thucydides, *The Peloponnesian War*, tr. Rex Warner. (London, Penguin Books, 1954). ISBN 0-14-044039-9.

— , *The Landmark Thucydides*, tr. Richard Crawley. (New York, The Free Press/Touchstone Books, 1996). pb. ISBN 0-68-482790-5; hb. ISBN 0-68-482815-4.

The passage of Thucydides we read is fairly small — to get a good feel for him as an historian one would want to read a good deal more. His entire history is a marvel of steely writing and very tight analysis. Warner's translation, like the preceding Herodotus, is a classic standby, and is fairly faithful to the Greek.

The Landmark Thucydides is based on the celebrated Richard Crawley translation, somewhat older than Warner's but generally considered one of the best. The edition is remarkable in having maps every few pages that clarify the historiographical task of the book. In paper or hardback, however, it is a good deal more expensive than the Penguin edition.

Plato, *The Collected Dialogues of Plato*, ed. Edith Hamilton and Huntington Cairns; tr. various. (Princeton, Princeton/Bollingen, 2nd. Ed., 1963). ISBN 0-69-109718-6.

— , *Complete Works*, ed. John M. Cooper and D. S. Hutchinson (Indianapolis, Hackett Pub. Co., 1997). ISBN 0-87-220349-2.

With Plato there are literally hundreds of editions and translations to which one can refer. Collections of different dialogues have been formed and reformed, coalescing around different purposes and questions, and sometimes without any guiding principles, with and without commentaries. Here I cite only a pair of complete Plato collections; one somewhat older, and one newer (and reputedly better). The Hamilton/Cairns edition has been a standard for many years, but it includes translations of varying quality and age, some of them going back to the occasionally awkward nineteenth-century versions of Benjamin Jowett. The more recent collection has more flexible and colloquial usage, and is probably easier to read.

*

Julius Caesar *The Conquest of Gaul*, tr. S. A. Hanford, rev. ed. (London, Penguin Books 1983). ISBN 0-14-044433-5.

Another standard entry into the Penguin Classics library, translating *The Gallic War*.

Cicero *Epistles*.

There really is no widely available edition of Cicero's letters currently in print for the non-specialist (in a reasonably-priced English translation). I would recommend looking at a library; for what we have in this course, though, one could reasonably print off the pair of letters from the web document.

Polybius, *The Rise of the Roman Empire,* tr. Ian Scott-Kilvert (London, Penguin Books, 1980). ISBN 0-14-044362-2.

This is somewhat abridged: the full Polybius is fairly lengthy.

Lucretius, *The Way Things Are,* tr. Rolfe Humphries (London/ Bloomington, University of Indiana, 1968). ISBN 0-25-320125-X.

— , *On the Nature of the Universe,* tr. R. E. Latham (London, Penguin Books, 1951). ISBN 0-14-044610-9.

Humphries' version is a long-time favorite translation of Lucretius' peculiar and challenging poem into fairly energetic English blank verse, faithful to Lucretius' sense. If the poetic form doesn't get in your way, I definitely recommend it. The Latham is a prose translation of the same work; perhaps easier for some to read, though not nearly as elegantly finished as the Humphries.

Catullus, *The Poems of Catullus,* tr. Peter Whigham (London, Penguin Books, 1966). ISBN 0-14-044180-8.

— , *Odi et Amo,* tr. Roy Arthur Swanson (Indianapolis, Bobbs-Merrill, 1959). ISBN 0-672-60314-4.

As I warned above, any complete translation of Catullus is going to contain material that many families are not going to want to have around the house. At his best, his poetry is brilliant, but a significant percentage of it is graphically and crudely sexual. With that in mind, I can also say that I have yet to see a published translation that really captures what's good about the original poetry. The Penguin listed here is for the sake of completeness: it's not particularly good; the Swanson is somewhat better in terms of accuracy, but still only so-so, to my own sense of things.

Horace, *The Odes and Epodes of Horace*, tr. Joseph P. Clancy (Chicago, University of Chicago, 1960). ISBN 0-22-610679-9.

— , *The Complete Odes and Epodes*, tr. W. G. Shepherd (London, Penguin Books, 1983). ISBN 0-14-044422-X.

— , *The Complete Odes and Epodes*, tr. David West (Oxford, OUP World's Classics, 1997). ISBN 0-19-283246-8.

— , *Horace in English*, ed. Kenneth Haynes and D. S. Carne-Ross, (London, Penguin Books, 1996). ISBN 0-14-042387-7.

Horace is as difficult to translate as any Latin poet. The architecture of his verse, his complexity of vocabulary, and the curious precision of his expression, all set a very high hurdle for the aspiring translator. None truly captures the perfection of Horace's poetry. Clancy's translation has stood the test of some time, however. West's translation (into verse, unlike his *Aeneid* we use for the class), is good, though a little free in spots. I have included the Penguin volume for reference, but have not yet been able to consult it.

I should repeat here the same warning I offered for Catullus: there are some rather crude poems among Horace's works — fewer than in Catullus, but they are there.

Horace in English is one of a series of volumes in the Penguin library that assembles various translations of a given poet created by the great translators of the last five hundred years or so. It is not a complete Horace, but it contains a number of excellent translations of individual works, some represented several times, displaying the variety of expression that Horace can support.

Ovid, *Metamorphoses*, tr. Allen Mandelbaum. (New York, Harcourt Brace/Harvest Books, reprint 1995). ISBN 0-14-044137-9.

—, *Metamorphoses*, tr. Rolfe Humphries. (Bloomington, Indiana University, 1955). ISBN 0-25-320001-6.

Mandelbaum is one of the great translators; his version of the *Metamorphoses* is certainly one of the best out there. It puts Ovid's agenda first, delivering the story in a sinewy blank verse with a rich and colorful vocabulary. It is very readable, but still captures some of the lushness of Ovid's diction — highly recommended to those who want to pursue the poem further. Humphries' version is plainer, but direct, accurate, and easy to read — rather like his Lucretius.

Other editions are available, including the Arthur Golding version from the mid-1500s, and another famous one assembled by a committee of Restoration poets including John Dryden — but these are more interesting, probably, as comments on the society that produced the translations than as windows onto Ovid's world.

Livy, *The Early History of Rome*, tr. Aubrey de Sélincourt, reprint ed. (London, Penguin Books, 1991). ISBN 0-14-044104-2.

Another very standard translation; very readable and reliable. Other sections of Livy appear in the other volumes of the set: this contains only Books I-V.

Augustine, *Confessions of St. Augustine*, tr. John Kenneth Ryan (Garden City, Image Books, 1960). ISBN 0-38-502955-1.

This is a good basic translation of the *Confessions*. In fact most of the translations of the *Confessions* I have consulted tend to be at least adequate: Augustine's language is not peculiarly rich, and he is not especially hard to translate into sound English prose. Any of the others available, save those that are particularly old (and hence archaic) are probably just about as good.

Benedict of Nursia, *Rule of St. Benedict*, tr. Anthony C. Meisel and M. L. del Mastro (Garden City, Image Books, 1975). ISBN 0-38-500948-8.

A satisfactory basic translation of a utilitarian, though brilliantly conceived, work.

Boëthius, *The Consolation of Philosophy*, rev. ed., tr. Victor Watts (London, Penguin Books, 1999). ISBN 0-14-044780-6.

A decent translation of a difficult work. Recommended, though with the caution that Boëthius is not particularly easy to translate in the best of times.

Gregory of Tours, *History of the Franks*, tr. Lewis Thorpe (London, Penguin Books, 1974). ISBN 0-14-044295-2.

The only complete modern translation I have discovered of Gregory's very idiosyncratic work. No translator could hope to capture the peculiar cragginess of the original without perhaps resorting to hillbilly English, and even then it wouldn't quite work. This gets the job done plainly by telling the story, and moving on.

Chrétien de Troyes, *Arthurian Romances*, tr. William W. Kibler and Carleton W. Carroll (London, Penguin Books, 1991). ISBN 0-14-044521-8.

— , *The Complete Romances of Chrétien de Troyes*, tr. David Staines (Bloomington, Indiana University, 1990). ISBN 0-25-320787-8.

These are both complete and reasonably modern prose translations of the romances, including the fragmentary *Perceval*, often omitted in earlier versions. I slightly prefer the Staines (and its spacious typeset is easier on the eyes). I have yet to discover verse translations of the complete *Romances*.

BACKGROUND

None of what follows is in any way required. I offer these titles
merely to supply the appetite of those who are really taken with early
literature, and want to pursue topics further along these lines. They
include texts from a wide range and of differing value. I've tried to
indicate something about each — why and how it might be useful, as
well as (where I'm competent to say) their relative strengths and
weaknesses. In no sense should the following list be considered even
remotely complete, however: there are great gaps that I've not even
attempted to fill. At the same time, it's all beyond the bounds of the
course proper. I've mostly tried to concentrate on the large pivotal
authors and to suggest some readings that would convey something
about both the nature of current scholarship and the depth of the field,
and also to express some of my own preferences. The following lists
are arranged in order of progression through the course.

Gregory Nagy, *The Best of the Achaeans* (Baltimore/London, Johns Hop-
kins, 1979). ISBN 0-80-182388-9.

A fairly technical study of the Homeric poems in terms of how
they are put together and the ideas they express, but containing
many exceedingly useful ideas, well-rooted in a sound philological
perspective. Nagy is (or was recently) the chairman of Harvard's
Classics department. I don't share all his ideas about the traditional
composition of certain kinds of poetry, but his views deserve to be
weighed very carefully.

H. D. F. Kitto, *Greek Tragedy*, (London, Methuen, 1939). ISBN 0-41-668900-0.

A solid introductory discussion of the field, though some of it is arguably rather dated.

Anne Pippin Burnett, *Catastrophe Survived: Euripides' Plays of Mixed Reversal*, (Oxford, OUP, 1971). ISBN 0-19-814038-X.

A controversial discussion, still not accepted everywhere, of a subset of Euripides' plays including the *Alcestis*, *Iphigenia in Tauris*, *Helen*, *Ion*, and *Andromache*. Not particularly relevant to something like *The Bacchae* at all, but an interesting view on Euripides' approach.

Francis Macdonald Cornford, *Before and After Socrates*, (London, Cambridge University, 1932). ISBN 0-52-109113-6.

Still one of the finest expositions, in the space of very few pages, of what Socrates (and Plato) accomplished in the history of ideas.

W. K. C. Guthrie, *The Greek Philosophers*, (New York, HarperCollins, 1986 [repr. of London, Methuen, 1950]). ISBN 0-06-131008-5.

A very sound introduction to the history of Greek philosophy, and Greek modes of thought. Guthrie also put together a massive series of volumes on Greek philosophy, but it's probably a good idea to read this one first.

Kenneth Quinn, *The Catullan Revolution* (Ann Arbor, University of Michigan, 1971 [repr. of Melbourne, 1959]). ISBN 0-47-206175-5.

Kenneth Quinn was probably the foremost Catullus scholar in the world, and his work has never been entirely supplanted. At its best, it is remarkably good — all the more noteworthy for the fact that a great deal of drivel has been published about Catullus in the last half century.

Brooks Otis, *Virgil, A Study in Civilized Poetry* (Norman/London, University of Oklahoma, 1995 [repr. of Oxford, OUP, 1964]). ISBN 0-80-612782-1.

A classic study of Vergil, especially the *Aeneid*, by a moderate and reasonable scholar. I do not agree with all his points, but his overall understanding of Vergil is profound and deeply informed, and his grasp on the structural issues at stake is first-rate. I use the book in my fourth-year Latin course.

Kenneth Quinn, *Virgil's* Aeneid: *A Critical Description*. (Ann Arbour [*sic*], University of Michigan, 1968). ISBN 0-52-003848-7

Kenneth Quinn, whose most influential study has been on Catullus, here brings considerable focus to Vergil as a poet.

W. R. Johnson, *Darkness Visible: A Study of Vergil's* Aeneid. (Berkeley, University of California,1976). ISBN 0-52-003848-7.

A much more recent study of Vergil's *Aeneid*, from a somewhat more pessimistic point of view than Otis, but again argued from a solid footing in the text, and to good effect. Undergirds many of my own perspectives on the poem.

Wendell Clausen, *Virgil's* Aeneid *and the Tradition of Hellenistic Poetry* (Berkeley, University of California, 1987). ISBN 0-52-005791-0.

   Clausen understands (and expresses) as clearly as anyone in the field the dependence of Vergil on his Hellenistic antecedents. He elsewhere ties the *Aeneid* in with Homer, of course, but here he shows how his poem is of a piece with the largely uncelebrated po- ets of the Hellenistic period, and how they in turn had their own peculiar perspectives on Homer. This requires some careful reading, but it's a marvelous book with a lot of mature depth.

Michael Putnam, *Virgil's Epic Designs: Ekphrasis in the* Aeneid (New Haven, Yale, 1998). ISBN 0-30-007353-4.

   Putnam's writing style is, to my taste, unduly obfuscated and falsely technical, but he does go into the whole problem of *ecphrasis* in some detail — and probably pays as much attention as has ever been given to the *ecphrases* of the *Aeneid* itself. Proceed with some caution, however.

Steele Commager, *The Odes of Horace: A Critical Study*, (Norman/ London, University of Oklahoma, 1995 [repr. of New Haven, Yale, 1962]). ISBN 0-80-612729-5.

   One of the more level-headed looks at Horace.

Eduard Fraenkel, *Horace*. (Oxford, Oxford University, 1957 [repr. of New Haven, Yale, 1962]). ISBN 0-19-814310-9.

   Probably the standard work on Horace; Fraenkel is discerning and intelligent.

Joseph Solodow, *The World of Ovid's* Metamorphoses. (Chapel Hill/ London, Univ. of N. Carolina). ISBN 0-80-781771-6.

A vexing book, but vexing for some of the same reasons Ovid's poem is vexing: it advances the intriguing thesis that there really is no thematic center or direction to the *Metamorphoses*. An interesting case study in argument from silence (or lack of perception), but hard to refute unless one can come up with something else.

L. D. Reynolds and N. G. Wilson, *Scribes and Scholars: A Guide to the Transmission of Greek and Latin Literature,* 3rd ed. (Oxford, OUP, 1991). ISBN 0-19-872146-3.

A now-classic study of the ways in which books traveled and texts were transmitted in the Middle Ages: a fascinating though rather detailed work.

W. P. Ker, *Epic and Romance.* (London, Macmillan and Co., 1897). No ISBN.

A now dated but broadly synthetic look at the nature and composition of mediaeval literature, and in particular the dichotomy between epic and romance forms — and the difficulty of keeping the two clearly separate. Out of print but likely available in many libraries.

C. S. Lewis, *The Discarded Image* (London, Cambridge University Press, 1964). ISBN 0-52-109450-X.

A fascinating and informative book about the basics of the mediaeval world-view, and the underpinnings of the literary world.

Erich Auerbach, *Dante: Poet of the Secular World*, tr. Ralph Manheim, with an introduction by Michael Dirda. (New York, New York Review of Books, 2007). ISBN 1-59-017219-3.

Auerbach's groundbreaking work on Dante, originally published in German as *Dante als Dichter der irdischen Welt* in 1929, is now happily back in print in English. It remains an energetic and insightful look at the work as a whole.

SPECIALIZED VOCABULARY: A GLOSSARY

ARISTEIA: In Homeric poetry, especially the *Iliad*, the *aristeia* is the moment of being the best (*aristos*) — a hero's moment in the sun, so to speak. Much of the earlier part of the *Iliad* is in fact made up of such passages, in which one hero after another becomes temporarily ascendant. Does this reflect that the *Iliad* is a conglomerate poem, made up of various *aristeiai* originally written independently and then stitched together, or is the distribution of glory in itself part of the intrinsic perspective of the Homeric poet's stock in trade? Nobody is really completely sure about the answer to this question, but as a unit of analysis and an explanation for the curiously episodic nature of much of the *Iliad* (as well as some other later poems) this rationale makes some sense.

CHANSON DE GESTE: In mediaeval French, the term *chanson de geste* refers to a long (epic, on some definitions) poem written in rhyming or assonant verse, concerned with the actions of historical or legendary figures.

CHTHONIC: "Of the earth" — having to do with a primarily feminine, earth-bound, material, and emotional/irrational principle. Typically expressed in earth-mother goddesses and blood sacrifices. In anthropology and myth/folklore analysis, the term is typically opposed to *uranic, q.v.*

COMEDY: In the narrow sense, a comedy is a dramatic form like the tragedy: its name does not necessarily prescribe anything very particular about its content, though there is a very high correlation

150

(much higher than that of content typical of tragedy, to be sure). We do not read any comedy in this course: the bulk of surviving Greek and Roman comedy varies from the mildly bawdy to the very crude. It's still worth knowing that it's out there, however.

ECPHRASIS: An *ecphrasis* (sometimes seen also as *ekphrasis*) is a "telling-out" — in ancient literary usage, an extended description (running from several lines to many pages) of some physical artifact, usually one that itself contains or suggests a story. Ecphrasis can first be found in Homer's *Iliad*, in perhaps its purest form in the so-called *Shield of Achilles* passage from Bk. XVIII; but as a technique it re-emerges in later Greek epic, in Vergil's *Aeneid*, in Ovid's *Metamorphoses*, in Catullus' C. 64 (the *epyllion* on the wedding of Peleus and Thetis), and a number of other occasions. As a device it is not yet dead: one can find patterns like it in "The Doubloon", chapter 100 (or so — editions vary) of Herman Melville's *Moby Dick*, or the section of Umberto Eco's *The Name of the Rose* describing the church doorway.

EPIC: In ancient Greek and Latin usage, *epic* was a kind of poetry written in dactylic hexameter relating the deeds of gods and heroes. In the intervening years, the term has come to apply to any national or ethnic heroic poetry, whether in hexameter or not, and recently has been applied willy-nilly to novels and films. In general, we will draw the line after the second definition, limiting the term to strictly poetic products, but in any of a variety of languages and metrical forms.

EPYLLION: The idea of a "baby epic" seems to have taken shape largely in response to the poetic theories of Callimachus, though we are still unclear as to whether anyone ever wrote a true *epyllion* or what it

looked like. If some scholars are right in their surmises, the late Hellenistic and neoteric Roman poets may have produced a few of these,
of which Catullus' C. 64 may be an example. That poem has a certain
claim to being a "baby epic", at any rate, since it runs to only a few
hundred lines, but is written about the deeds of heroes and gods in
dactylic hexameter. It takes (via a narrow glimpse at the wedding
feast of Peleus and Thetis) a look at the larger material of Homeric
epic, since Peleus and Thetis were the parents of Achilles; an anti-
thetical theme is introduced through the *ecphrasis* on the coverlet,
which relates the story of the failed marriage of Ariadne, abandoned
by Theseus on Naxos.

GOSPEL: The term "gospel" is derived from Old English *godspell*, a literal and direct translation of the Latin/Greek term *evangelium*, which
means "good news". The term came, of course, to apply to the narratives of the life, ministry, teachings, death, and resurrection of Christ.
Out of a larger number, four were determined to be canonical and
deserving of attention.

HYPOTAXIS: In grammatical or stylistic description, the construction of
sentences characterized by a large number of subordinate clauses,
usually leading to a hierarchically-ordered periodic sentence, as opposed to *parataxis, q.v.*

KLEOS: *Kleos* is the fundamental coin of Homeric heroic culture: it is
fame, presumably eternal, conferred upon the hero by those who
come afterward (especially the poet, whose job it is to sing the *klea
andron*). The quest for *kleos* will cost Achilles his life: he must choose
between winning *kleos* and the possibility of *nostos*, a homecoming.

He eventually chooses the former, and dies at Troy. The choice is seen as in some ways representative or even typical of the choices facing a hero on the Homeric model; the *Odyssey* does, however, offer an alternative possibility.

LYRIC: Lyric poetry is, in general, poetry intended to be sung, most often to a lyre or similar instrument. Its cultural analogue today is probably the popular tune sung to the accompaniment of a guitar. Then as now, this seemingly simple definition hides a world of complexity and almost infinite variety. In fact, the poetry that is categorized as lyric in the ancient world tended to be of a very specific type, not too long, and characterized by a certain range of poetic meters. Lyric poems tended to be stanzaic (composed in chunks of lines with unique metrical demands, of about four lines each) rather than stichic (composed in a regular single-line pattern). The great lyric poets of the Greek world were fairly early — before the fifth century "Golden Age" — and include Sappho, Alcaeus, Archilochus, Stesichorus, and even the Athenian head of state Solon. The Latin poets found this metrically challenging and appealing, and so Latin poetry also has similar figures and types — the best-known Latin lyric poets being Catullus and Horace.

MENIPPEAN SATIRE: Menippean satire, which goes back to middle republican Roman writings, is not nearly as complex as the label that's been given it. It is something in which passages of prose alternate with passages of verse, often in a variety of different meters. The one example we read here is the *Consolation of Philosophy* of Boëthius.

NEOTEROI, NEOTERIC POETS: The word *neoteroi* merely means "newer" in Greek; it referred at Rome to the "new poets" of the generation from Catullus through Vergil, who patterned their aesthetics on the ideas of Callimachus. Not everyone bought into the package: Cicero, for example, occasionally derided them, and labeled them with the still-not-quite-clear tag *cantores Euphorionis*.

NOSTOS: The word from which we get our "nostalgia", *nostos* refers primarily in this course to the homecoming of the Greek heroes. It becomes a point of reference in a kind of polar opposition between two extremes being contrasted with *kleos*, and in this regard gives us some one tool to unlock the moral universe of heroic-age Greek.

PARATAXIS: In grammatical or stylistic description, the construction of sentences characterized chiefly by independent or coordinate clauses, usually stylistically fairly simple, as opposed to *hypotaxis*, *q.v.*

PROPEMPTICON: A "sending-off" — that is, in poetic usage, a kind of *"bon voyage"* poem. The chief example (and the only one we look at in this course) is Horace, *Odes* I.3, addressed to Vergil (*Sic te diva potens Cypri*).

PSALM: The Psalms are a peculiarly Hebrew form of poetry; and though they are apparently quite laced with puns and other tricks of sound, they are dependent for their most basic poetic form less on any particular acoustical features (*e.g.,* rhyme, rhythm, etc.) than upon an alternation or bipartite echo of *ideas*. The verses tend to be responsorial in that the second part will typically either restate the ideas of the first in parallel terms, or affirm them by denying the opposite, or proceed using some conspicuously contrasting form of symbolism. As such, the Psalms are oddly suited to translation.

RECUSATIO: A "polite refusal" — in Roman poetry of the first century, it was an almost established form in which the poet protests his inability to write epic. The most clever instances of this sort of thing play both sides of the fence: in refusing to write the epic (and by way of protest) the poet also introduces epic themes and shows that in fact, he probably *would* be able to pull it off if he were so inclined. Chiefly Horatian.

RHAPSODE: The early Homeric bard is sometimes called a *rhapsode*, though the term does not appear in the Homeric poems themselves. The relationship of the poet to the hero is discussed somewhat in both the Homeric poems and in other works, like the Odes of Pindar.

ROMANCE: The *romance* as a mediaeval form is chiefly distinguished from epic in its tone and the flexibility of its medium. Romances could be written in either prose or poetry; they tended to be somewhat shorter than epics, but tonally somewhat less serious. Often they were adorned with fantastical elements, and, though the presence of what we now consider the "romantic" element — i.e., having to do with romantic love — it does not preclude this option either. A good many romances did have to do with courtly love, and the largest number seem to have arisen around the Arthurian mythos, which penetrated almost every country in Western Europe aside from Spain. This course includes only one real romance in the classic mold — that being the *Yvain* of Chrétien de Troyes — but in many ways the romance tradition also leaves its mark on such things as the *Nibelungenlied*, which is probably still to be considered an epic, and in a large sense, Dante's *Divine Comedy* itself can perhaps best be seen as a kind of grand romance.

SAGA: The term saga is (like "epic") used very loosely in popular parlance nowadays, but properly it refers to *prose* narratives of the Old Norse tradition (usually containing scraps of poetry, but never wholly poetic). The form routinely encompasses a number of generations of a single family, thus preventing us from forming any clear notion of a single main character; the narrative structure may be rather amorphous, as well. Still, as a form it was characteristic of the northern countries (most particularly Iceland) and some of the sagas (most notably the *Volsunga Saga* and the *Thidrek's Saga*) preserve pieces of the most primitive stories of the early Germanic migration — including the tales surrounding Sigurd (Siegfried in the German versions), which are of a piece with both the *Nibelungenlied* on one hand and the *Hildebrandslied* on the other.

TRAGEDY: The origin and significance of the term ("goat-song") is obscure, and how it grew out of cultic practice is similarly unclear, but the term tends to denote a play of serious content, not necessarily with an unhappy ending, but usually not comic in any way, in which there are fairly few actors and extensive periods of choral song and dance according to a fairly well-established formula. The nearest modern analogy in content might well be the musical, though the notion of musical *comedy* would certainly be missing. The plays tended to be larded with fairly difficult philosophical and theological notions, and were viewed widely by the audiences of Athens.

URANIC: "Of the sky" — having to do with a primarily masculine, heavenly, formal, and rational principle. Typically expressed in male sky divinities. In anthropology and myth/folklore analysis, the term is typically opposed to *chthonic, q.v.*

Timeline

1500 BC		
1400 BC	Abraham[?]	
1300 BC		
1200 BC	Approx. date, Exodus	Approx. date, Trojan War
1100 BC		
1000 BC	David on throne of Israel	
900 BC		
800 BC	800-500 BC.: So-called Lyric Age of Greece	**"Homer"**; Homeric poems
700 BC		753 BC. Traditional founding of Rome
600 BC		
500 BC		
	500-400 BC: Golden Age Athens	**Aeschylus**, ca. 525-456 BC; **Sophocles**, 496-06 BC; **Euripides**, 480-06 BC; **Herodotus**, 485-425 BC; **Thucydides**, 460-400 BC; **Socrates**, ca. 470-399 BC.
400 BC		
	Alexander the Great, 336-323 BC.	**Plato** 427-347 BC. Aristotle, 384-322 BC.
300 BC		
200 BC	Alexandrian scholar/poet Callimachus, third cent. BC	
100 BC	150 BC-AD 17: Golden Age of Roman Literature 44 BC, Death of Caesar 31 BC-AD 17, rule of Augustus; beginning of Empire	**Cicero**, ca 106-42 BC; **Caesar**, ca 100-44 BC, **Lucretius**, ca 96-55 BC, **Catullus**, ca 84-ca 54 BC.
–	ca AD 30, Ministry, death, and resurrection of Jesus	**Vergil**, ca 70-19 BC; **Horace**, ca 65-8 BC; **Livy** ca. 59 BC-AD 17; **Ovid**, ca 43 BC-AD 17
AD 100	ca AD 65, Death of **Paul**	
AD 200		
AD 300	Diocletian persecuting Christians, splits Empire 285	
	Constantine legalizes Christianity in Roman Empire 312	
AD 400		**Augustine of Hippo**, 354-430
	Vandals sack Rome, 410	

AD 500		
		Boëthius, ca 480-524;
AD 600		**Benedict of Nursia**, ca 480-547;
AD 700		**Gregory of Tours**, 538-594
AD 800	Charlemagne crowned Holy Roman Emperor, Christmas 800	**Anon. Hildebrandslied**, ca 800
AD 900		
AD 1000		**Anon. Song of Roland**, ca 1000
AD 1100		
AD 1200	"Renaissance of the Twelfth Century"	**Chretien de Troyes** fl. 1160-75
		Anon. Nibelungenlied, ca 1200-1215
		Anon. Volsunga Saga, ca. 1200-1270
AD 1300		**Thomas Aquinas**, 1225-1274
		Dante Alighieri, 1264-1321
		Dante's Vision Easter 1300
AD 1400	1348: Black Death reaches Europe	Francesco Petrarcha, Italian Humanist
AD 1500	Columbus discovers America, 1492	
AD 1600		
AD 1700		
AD 1800	American Independence, 1776	
AD 1900	US Civil War, 1861-1864 World War I: 1914-1918	
AD 2000	World War II: 1939-1945 **1995: Western Literature to Dante first taught**	

159

6417432R0

Made in the USA
Lexington, KY
18 August 2010